Foreign Policy for America in the Twenty-first Century

T0123876

Edited by **Thomas H. Henriksen**

Foreign Policy for America in the Twenty-first Century

Alternative Perspectives

Hoover Institution Press Stanford University Stanford, California

Hoover Institution Press Publication No. 491

Copyright © 2001 by the Board of Trustees of the
   Leland Stanford Junior University

First printing, 2001
06   05   04   03   02   9   8   7   6   5   4   3   2

Manufactured in the United States of America

The paper used in this publication meets the minimum requirements
of American National Standard for Information Sciences—Permanence
of Paper for Printed Library Materials, ANSI Z39.48–1984. ⊗

Library of Congress Cataloging-in-Publication Data

Foreign policy for America in the twenty-first century : alternative perspectives /
edited by Thomas H. Henriksen.
        p.   cm. — (Hoover Institution Press publication ; no. 491)
     Includes bibliographical references and index.
     ISBN 0-8179-2792-1 (alk. paper)
     1. United States—Foreign relations—1989–   2. United States—Foreign
relations—21st century—Forecasting.   I. Henriksen, Thomas. H.   II. Series.
E840 .F677   2001
327.73—dc21   2001016832

Contents

Preface

The decade since the Soviet Union's unraveling has spawned conflicting perspectives on America's role in the world. The United States now
finds itself the sole superpower with vast economic, political, diplomatic, and military resources. Scholars, government officials, and a few
media professionals have contributed to the debate on how America
should utilize its unprecedented influence. Their opinions are found
in books, journals, serious magazines, and the elite press. But major
schools of thought or broad philosophical outlooks on the subject of
foreign affairs remain the preserve of a few policy wonks in and out of
government, plus a few news junkies in the general public.

The absence of a clear and present danger contributes to this lack
of attention. The splendid economic well-being of many Americans
exacerbates it further. But from history we know that peaceful and
prosperous epochs come to an end. Sometimes an international threat
grabs attention. At other times, an economic downturn has concentrated public interest on policy issues. The editor of this volume and
its contributors firmly hold that even in good times America is most
secure with an informed citizenry. We hope that this slender volume,
offering clashing opinions on America's international role, will advance the discussion of the subject.

Given the recent presidential campaign as well as the self-exami-
nation that comes with the genesis of a new century, attention turns to

what course the United States should sail. Each of this volume's contributors embraces a different vision of what U.S. foreign policy should
be in the opening decades of the twenty-first century.

In the introductory chapter, "From the Berlin Wall's Collapse to
the Present," Thomas Henriksen reviews briefly some of the salient
features of the decade following the collapse of the Soviet Union. His
purpose is to lay out the major crises in the international landscape
after the demise of America's greatest adversary. He calls attention to
the so-called rogue states, the engagement of China, and the decline
of Russian power. He places America's search for a post-Soviet policy
within a historical context and the current globalization phenomena.
The overview is designed to provide the general reader with enough
background information to make sense of arguments laid out in the
balance of the book.

John Lewis Gaddis reviews the need and desirability of a grand
strategy for the post–Cold War world. Although such a strategy may
seem unnecessary now, he points out the transience of the current
historical moment, the utility of balancing resources against a measur-
able plan, and the benefits of thinking about statecraft in as disciplined
a way as possible.

In Gaddis's view, thinking carefully about foreign policy is more
likely to spare us a calamity than reacting to case-by-case dilemmas. He
advises that we as a nation think clearly about our strategic destination,
minimize resistance to our goals, and plan rather than improvise a
strategy.

Writing in support of multilateralism, Richard Falk calls attention
to what he perceives as a paradox in American foreign policy—the
nation's desire to spread democracy to individual countries yet reluc-
tance to implement democracy at a global institutional level. Professor
Falk advocates making international organizations such as the United
Nations a higher priority. The next president ought to strengthen the
American public's confidence in collective bodies. In Falk's view,
Washington has failed to live up to its responsibilities as the UN's most

prominent member. He also proposes the creation of a global parliament within the UN.

According to Larry Diamond, promoting democracy in repressive states or sustaining beleaguered democratic governments ought to be *the* foreign policy thrust for the United States in the new century. Diamond emphasizes that never in world history has the political soil been more fertile for wedding the founding principles of America to its global strategy and power. He stresses that both American ideals and national interests call for the spread of liberal democracy around the globe.

Diamond argues that replacing dictatorships that nurture terrorism promotes our security as well as advances our values. Entrenching democracy, in his opinion, offers the best means to keeping the peace. Realizing an ambitious goal of world democracy requires that we marshal our resources, energy, imagination, and political leadership to the task, he says.

For decades, most economists have linked a nation's economic growth with trade liberalization. But a smaller number have countered that developing economies ought to be protected from foreign competition. Sebastian Edwards takes up the debate in light of antiglobalization protestors, who say that free trade disproportionately harms poor states. Citing other economists and his own empirical research, Edwards demonstrates that openness to trade and financial investment reduces poverty and improves the social conditions of developing countries. Thus, the United States must continue to promote free trade.

Americans have less interest in international affairs in the wake of the Soviet Union's disintegration. Judging from history, Thomas Henriksen urges Washington to buck the isolationist currents that have engulfed the two major political parties. In espousing a measured global activism, he recommends expanding the Asia Pacific Economic Cooperation forum into a fuller organization resembling the European

Union. He advocates a coalition effort to help defuse problems brewing in war-torn Afghanistan.

While favoring economic engagement with China, Henriksen cautions against excessive optimism regarding Beijing's intentions toward its neighbors. A neo-imperial Russia and a unifying Europe are altering the geopolitical environment in ways that demand Washington's attention. India's importance in the next century must also not be overlooked. Henriksen is wary of excessive realpolitik, believing that struggling for American values does not necessarily distract from the pursuit of our vital interests. Above all, he calls for a resolute foreign policy and a rebuilt military.

As a counterargument to overseas activism, Walter McDougall concludes with a spirited chapter that denies the need for a grand strategy in the post–Cold War world. McDougall opposes what he views as the neoliberal pursuit of economic globalization and democratic enlargement to secure American interests. He is also critical of the so-called neoconservative approach, which strives to establish an American "benevolent global hegemony."

McDougall calls for a cessation of crusades and urges instead the husbanding of assets for future crises. His list of assets includes a robust military, sturdy regional alliances, balances of power in Europe, the Middle East, and Asia. McDougall also espouses strong Pan-American institutions to fight threats posed by illegal immigrants and drugs.

The authors of this slender volume were selected not for their unanimity but for their conflicting visions. It is believed that these differing points of view reflect the nation's major outlooks at the dawn of America's third century. They are set forth with the Baconian inspiration that truth is more likely to emerge from error than from ignorance. They are advanced in this book in the belief that vigorous discussion is vital to the formulation of policy.

Acknowledgments

This volume would not have come to light had it not been for the encouragement and support of John Raisian, Director of the Hoover Institution, who backed it from conception to publication. I am also indebted to my research assistants, first to Piers Turner who helped conceive the scope of the book as well as provided early editing, and then to Jeanene Harlick who pulled the laboring oar in the editing phase. The contributors themselves embraced the project and wrote chapters with clearly stated but different viewpoints on foreign policy that will offer insights beyond the first crisis overseas. They willingly took to suggestions and made revisions. Patricia Baker, the Executive Editor of the Press, and Ann Wood, Senior Editor, worked diligently and expeditiously to turn the manuscript into a finished product.

Contributors

LARRY DIAMOND is a Senior Research Fellow at the Hoover Institution and coeditor of the *Journal for Democracy*. A prolific scholar, his most recent book is *Developing Democracy: Toward Consolidation*.

SEBASTIAN EDWARDS holds the Henry Ford II Chair in International Management Business in The John E. Anderson Graduate School of Management at the University of California, Los Angeles. He is widely published and his latest book is *Crisis and Reform in Latin America: From Despair to Hope*.

RICHARD A. FALK is the Albert G. Milbank Professor of International Law and Practice and professor of politics and international affairs at Princeton University. He is the author of *Law, War, and Morality in the Contemporary World* and *Law in an Emerging Global Village: A Post-Westphalian Perspective*.

JOHN LEWIS GADDIS is a Senior Fellow at the Hoover Institution and Robert Lovett Professor of History at Yale University. His awards include the Bancroft Prize and his most recent book is *We Now Know: Rethinking Cold War History*.

THOMAS H. HENRIKSEN is a Senior Fellow and Associate Director at the Hoover Institution. He has authored books and articles dealing with international affairs, revolution, and politics in Asia and Africa. His most recent monograph is entitled *Using Power and Diplomacy to Deal with Rogue States.*

WALTER A. MCDOUGALL is the Alloy-Ansin Professor of International Relations and professor of history at the University of Pennsylvania. He received the Pulitzer Prize for history for his book, *The Heavens and Earth: A Political History of the Space Age.* His most recent volume is *Promised Land, Crusader State: The American Encounter with the World since 1776.*

Thomas H. Henriksen

Introduction:
From the Berlin Wall's Collapse to the Present

Playing political musical chairs on a regional basis may be common, but power shuffles on a global scale are rare. Nations battle and make peace periodically; states rise to or fall from power, but none of these incidents shatters the world system. Thus, drastic shifts in worldwide alignment are really historic milestones.

The sudden demise of the USSR was such a change, and it left the United States in a global position without historical analogy. Never before has one state enjoyed such global reach. Neither the Roman nor the British empires—to name two frequently named predecessors—provide instructive precedent. The History Muse's admonition that the past is prologue is no use in this new global configuration.

Historical chapter-changes, in which one epoch ends and another begins, demand hard thinking about external affairs. But judging from history, nations generally do not examine their foreign relations unless confronted by a threat. Instead, they focus internally. The decade since the collapse of the Soviet Union has presented the United States with a string of low-order crises. Acting alone or with others, the United States confronted rogue regimes and intervened in several failed states more for humanitarian purposes than national interests. No comprehensive strategic vision took shape from inside the Clinton government despite an array of proposals floated by officials and by pundits. Instead, a series of intrastate upheavals in Rwanda, Haiti, and elsewhere grabbed headlines and focused the spotlight on Washington's ability to end civil strife, restore order, and care for the destitute.

A Brief Look Back

A glance at the past two centuries of world politics highlights the radically altered landscape on which the United States must now operate. The new global pecking order with the United States at the top contrasts starkly with past periods when intense international rivalries served to balance powerful states. From the end of the Napoleonic wars in 1815 to the outbreak of World War I, European alignments were stable—although the century-old system came under stress in the early twentieth century by Germany's rise to prominence and European imperial rivalry. Balance-of-power diplomacy within Europe deserves much credit for this century of peace.

When war broke out in 1914, it engulfed Europe, shattered the old order, led to the collapse of four monarchies (Russian, German, Austro-Hungarian, and Turkish sultan), and contributed to the rise of fascism and communism. In short, the war transformed the political and strategic order. It also paved the way for WWII and the Cold War division of the planet into Soviet and American camps, with a putative nonaligned bloc that tilted distinctly toward socialism.

Once established, the Cold War confrontation created a power standoff that allowed for four decades of somewhat predictable relations. The Soviet Union and the United States engaged in worldwide competition wherein each side strove to match the other—first in Central Europe and then in remote corners of the world. But neither side wanted to risk mutual destruction with a general war or a nuclear exchange. Despite tension and small wars on the world's periphery, the global chessboard remained frozen with only pawns consumed until the Soviet Union disintegrated, leaving the United States without a peer competitor.

The contrast between our new era and the Cold War period could hardly be drawn more sharply. In retrospect, the preceding East-West struggle appears the picture of clarity in its aims, whereas our current world seems ambiguous. During the Cold War, the containment doctrine aimed at confronting Soviet expansion. As such, it formed an organizing principle for over forty years of American foreign policy. Like most grand concepts, it witnessed lapses and setbacks but the policy itself endured and ultimately prevailed. Its broad acceptance, application to specific cases, and standard on which to match ends and means made containment an imaginative and effective national strategy. The United States found itself adrift when the Soviet Union collapsed, much like the team that prevails in a tug-of-war contest when its opponents let go of the rope.

Over the past century, the United States has responded unevenly to global power shifts that should have sparked a redefining of its foreign policy. For instance, America responded to the Spanish-American War, a relatively minor skirmish, by becoming more attentive to Asia, Central America, and the Caribbean. Later, the United States turned inward in the aftermath of World War I. In America's desire for a "return to normalcy," it left Europe and Asia alone to face fascism, communism, and other threats to international security.

Then, after World War II, in an about-face, Washington redefined its policy to give birth to the doctrine of containment. To confront Moscow, Washington negotiated alliances in Europe and Asia, economically assisted allies, and put in place a worldwide military presence. Likewise, the United States undertook policy revisions after the wars in Korea and Vietnam. The setback in the Southeast Asian conflict, for example, led to diplomatic engagement of China to bolster the United States against the Soviet Union.

When the Iron Curtain crumbled, U.S. policy vacillated once again. Faced with the greatest power shift in world history, the United States looked inward again in a post–WWI replay. Americans greeted the collapse of the Soviet Union with more of a collective sigh than with a triumphal cheer. Rather than look for fresh conquests, as imperial powers in the past, the United States cut its military budget, reduced its armed forces, and withdrew 200,000 troops from Europe. Domestic concerns captured attention. Americans focused on the economy, school reform, technological advances, and their own pursuits. Poll after poll canvassing American opinion recorded a dwindling interest beyond our shores.

During the decade following the crumbling of the Berlin Wall, the United States put a premium on economic internationalism. Among the achievements of this emphasis was the passage of the North American Free Trade Agreement, linking Canada, Mexico, and the United States in reducing tariffs to expand trade. Washington also pushed for creation of the World Trade Organization to nurture America's longstanding ends of multilateral trade, currency convertibility, and the free flow of capital. Worldwide economic development reflected America's belief that growth furthered its own prosperity and the cause of peace and democracy among nations. Globalization and economic integration alone fell short of a strategic agenda, however.

The result is that the United States entered the twenty-first century with unrivaled dominance but without a roadmap to guide its newfound role as the sole superpower. It encountered a string of outlaw regimes and dysfunctional states with bloody ethnic conflicts. None of these difficulties was of sufficient magnitude to threaten American vital interests or evoke a compelling paradigm shift. They failed to generate an overarching doctrine similar to the containment agenda of the Cold War era. Instead, international and domestic circumstances throw up competing approaches to the transformed world. Ten years after the demise of America's greatest foe, the United States searches for a policy toward the outside world that can be translated into clear guidelines. This volume is dedicated to further that search.

After the Fall of the Berlin Wall

The disintegration of the Iron Curtain unleashed a political gale that swept across the Eurasian chessboard, leaving confused and toppled players in wholly new positions. The tearing down of the Berlin Wall in 1989, which separated not only East and West Germany but also communist Eastern and democratic Western Europe, dramatically began the unraveling of the Soviet Union, which took place two years later in 1991.

The Red Army withdrew its garrisons from Eastern Europe, allowing democratically elected governments east of the Elbe River to rise to power and the two Germanys to reunify. The Soviet Union's demise itself precipitated the spawning of five central Asian states, the freeing of Armenia and Georgia, and the replacement of communist rule with democratic elections.

In Washington, the subsiding of nuclear tensions precipitated the hope for a peaceful epoch, wherein economic integration and diplomatic cooperation would usher in a golden age. Reality soon revealed the foolishness of this unrealistic optimism.

Several divisive issues clouded the hoped-for harmony of a strategic partnership between the two former Cold War adversaries. Whereas Washington imagined Russia in a subordinate relationship, much like Germany and Japan after 1945, Moscow saw its destiny through a different prism. For half a millennium, Russia had been a major power in the councils of Europe. Its expectations were that history would continue to run the same course.

Moreover, Russia and the United States were still at cross purposes over specific disputes ranging from the Baltics, the Balkans, and Chechen separatism, to NATO enlargement and pipeline locations for natural gas and oil from Central Asia. While the American-Russian relationship bumped along on a less-threatening path, antagonisms still lingered.

The Return of China to the World Stage

In Asia, paradoxically, Russia's sudden decline contrasted sharply with China's economic rise. Although the Soviet Union's defeat upended the widely held conviction that the Red Army would never allow communism to fall from power, this surprising turn of events did not cause Chinese leadership to loosen its totalitarian grip over the country. On the contrary—and helped in no small part by foreign investors eyeing the country's market potential—Chinese nationalism soared as faith in communism flagged. The reemergence of China as regional power recalled its international position two centuries ago, contributing to Chinese pride and to their neighbors' unease.

Beijing laid claim to wide swaths of the South China Sea, secured the return of Hong Kong and Macao to Chinese rule, and asserted that Taiwan's status was an internal matter closed to interference from Washington. In 1996, it fired missiles to disrupt Taiwan's first direct presidential election. When the United States sent warships in response, China lined its coast with missile batteries as a signal of exclusive control. Since then, Beijing has added to its military strength through domestic production, Russian arms purchases, and U.S. nuclear technology.

Citing the catastrophic results of excluding pre-WWI Germany from the international community, people from both within and outside the U.S. government pushed to engage China economically and politically despite revulsion against the 1989 Tiananmen Square massacre and a persisting poor human-rights record. They argued that an economically liberalizing and modernizing society would gradually transform China into a full-fledged democracy as it had in Chile, South Korea, Spain, and Taiwan. Because containment of China ran counter to the course of globalization, the proponents held that no realistic option existed other than China's economic integration into the world economy.

Opponents, however, cautioned against excessive optimism about

China's democratic prospects. The skeptics called attention to China's ongoing human rights abuses, bellicose rants, and anti-American harangues. They demanded prudence in scientific and military interchanges, lest weapons-related technology fall into potentially hostile hands. Critics often advocated a defense commitment with Taiwan. The Sino-skeptics, in short, advocated that the United States, Japan, and Chinese neighbors keep their powder dry.

Rogue States Imperiled the New International Order

Russia's decline and China's rise generated flux in the international equilibrium. Threatening regimes and terrorist networks contributed to the turbulence. Anti-American terrorists, many under the tutelage of onetime Saudi Arabian businessman Osama bin Laden, struck at U.S. embassies and citizens. Although U.S. counterintelligence measures foiled many attacks, the prevalence of deadly threats contributed to unease and complicated relations with terrorist host states like Afghanistan, Iran, Pakistan, and the Sudan.

A far more marked global transformation, however, took place because of the antics of so-called rogue states (or "states of concern" as the Department of State renamed them last year). A handful of these pariah regimes were left to their own devices with the lifting of the Iron Curtain. They developed weapons of mass destruction and missile delivery systems, breached treaty-mandated inspections, and nurtured or launched terrorism against their adversaries. Iraq invaded Kuwait, North Korea armed itself with missiles and deadly weapons, the Sudan butchered its own citizens in the south, and Serbian leaders incited "ethnic cleansing" campaigns against Croats and Bosnian Muslims with the aim of creating a Greater Serbia.

During the Cold War era, these bad actors served Chinese and Soviet interests. But Moscow, while often aiding their violent measures, exercised a degree of restraint on their actions, lest they trigger superpower conflict. With Moscow's fall, rogues like Iraq and North Korea slipped their Soviet leash. These states have now achieved a notoriety of their own making. How to deal with these international outlaws, who have perfected the black arts of terrorism and mass murder, present still-unresolved dilemmas for the United States and its allies.

Iraq

Rather than licking its wounds after the Gulf War, a defeated Iraq placed itself beyond the pale of the international community by secretly engaging in nuclear weapons production, biological warfare research, and contravening international arms control agreements. An appalling human rights record and ongoing threats to neighboring Kuwait round out the Iraqi profile as the quintessential rogue regime, rivaled only by North Korea for the most notorious rank.

Backed by Washington but hobbled by China, France, and Russia, the United Nations Security Council strove to inspect Iraqi facilities for the manufacture of weapons of mass destruction. After the thirty-nation coalition liberated Kuwait, the United Nations imposed trade sanctions against Iraq until all of its nuclear, chemical, and biological weapons could be located and destroyed. But Baghdad frustrated UN Special Commission inspection teams. Finally, UNSCOM pulled out of Iraq. Saddam Hussein sought to increase oil exportation, using the resulting hard currency to further weapons acquisitions rather than alleviate the hunger and medical needs of the country's destitute population. Hussein's roguery was calculated to dominate the Persian Gulf, intimidate his neighbors, and threaten U.S. allies in the region.

North Korea

Across the globe, North Korean maneuvers further unbalanced the international equilibrium. The Stalinist regime north of the thirty-eighth parallel owed its origin and ideological rigidity to the bitter divisions of the Cold War. As the Cold War lengthened, some communist states gradually softened their wholesale repression and searched for limited market solutions to economic backwardness. North Korea, however, remained frozen in a time warp that dated from the Korean War (1950–1953). Pyongyang matched its internal cruelty with international terrorist incidents. Its ideological rigidity coincided with China's economic liberalization, making North Korea less compatible with its neighbor.

North Korea lost its chief source of foreign assistance with the Soviet breakup. To compensate, it adopted a "shakedown" strategy designed to bully its foes to cough up food and other material aid—much-needed relief for shortages due to a cycle of drought and floods.

In 1993, Pyongyang threatened to reprocess weapons-grade plutonium from an aging nuclear reactor, alarming South Korea, Japan, and the United States. Such nuclear production constituted a breach in the Nonproliferation Treaty, which Pyongyang had signed in 1985. By late spring 1994, the United States and North Korea appeared on the brink of conflict.

To resolve the crisis, the Clinton administration entered into an elaborate arrangement with Pyongyang. In return for a promise to freeze its nuclear program, North Korea received pledges from the United States, Japan, and Korea to build first one and then another light-water nuclear reactor at a cost of $4 billion by early in this century. Washington agreed to supply 500,000 metric tons of fuel oil until the new facilities came on line, but required that construction funds come from Tokyo, Seoul, and other sources. Later, the United States supplemented its fuel aid with foodstuffs that were distributed through the UN's World Food Program. This support made North Korea the top recipient of American aid in Asia after 1994.

Despite the agreement and beneficence, Pyongyang first constructed an underground complex near its nuclear center—stirring anew concerns of secret weapons and missile development — and then test-fired a multistage, solid-fuel rocket over northern Japan. These actions unnerved its neighbors and resulted in warnings from the

United States. A year later, in order to lessen tensions, Washington agreed to drop most of the economic sanctions imposed on North Korea after the Korean War. Pyongyang continued to rail against U.S. support for its southern neighbor but also gradually began to respond to diplomatic initiatives from Australia, Italy, and Japan. It also entered into economic agreements with a South Korean conglomerate to permit tourism. Finally, in mid-2000, North and South held a historic summit, which led to an intrapeninsula thaw.

Serbia

A special category of the rogue-state phenomenon is reserved for Serbia, the dominant political entity in the former Yugoslavia. Slobodan Milosevic's Serbia exhibited all the brutalities of the typical rogue nation. It engaged in genocide against non-Serbian peoples living in the Balkans—such as Bosnian Muslims and Croats. Serbs also killed thousands of Kosovo Albanians. But Serbia posed no direct military threat to neighboring states. Its ethnic cleansing campaigns roiled the region, if only by expelling hundreds of thousands of refugees from Serb-claimed lands. These ruthless campaigns ran the risk of engulfing the Balkans and drawing in neighboring states to quench the fires. But unlike Iraqi or North Korean provocations, Belgrade's policies were not interpreted by surrounding countries as border-crossing menaces. Mass murder was an in-house affair.

Nor did the Serbs embark on the construction of weapons of mass destruction or missile delivery systems for nuclear bombs or biological agents. Whereas North Korea, Iraq, and Iran sought out viruses, atoms, and rockets, Serbia eschewed these deadly instruments. Yet Milosevic threatened regional harmony with his campaign of ethnic cleansing. Following the Kosovo air campaign, the Serb strongman persisted in stirring ethnic hatred in the breakaway province. Before his ouster by democratic elements, Milosevic also jeopardized the autonomy of Montenegro, Serbia's sister republic in the former Yugoslavia. His fall from power in late 2000 gave hope to southeastern Europe for a less-turbulent future than the past decade but it left unresolved the fate of Kosovo.

Russia Stumbles on As a Fading Power

In Russia, the peaceful transfer of power cloaked the country's diminished position, obscuring the needed reforms appropriate for a defeated, bankrupt country. No Western armies garrisoned the vanquished state, tried or incarcerated its former leaders, or grafted democratic government onto its unraveling society, as the Allies did with Germany, Japan, and Italy at the end of WWII.

Instead, Russians dismantled their ruling communist regime, drafted a new constitution, elected candidates to office, and freed formerly captive peoples. Western intervention was limited to narrow technical and misplaced financial assistance.

Freed from centralized controls, the Soviet economy was exposed for what it was—a sheltered, backward-looking, metal-based industrial structure that could neither adapt nor reconstitute itself to face the fierce competition of the global information age. Thus, while China marched toward regional power status, Russia slid into near–Third World decrepitude.

Russia, in spite of its declining economy and conventional military strength, is still striving to maintain its former world standing. As its geopolitical power evaporated, Moscow has redoubled its diplomatic measures to frustrate American foreign policy goals by opposing NATO's eastward expansion, the Atlantic alliance's intervention in Bosnia and Kosovo, and more. Vladimir Putin, the globe-trotting president, travels to conventional nation-states and rogue countries alike to boost Russia's standing. He courts China to compensate for Russia's weakness against the United States while simultaneously competing with Beijing for influence in resource-rich Central Asia.

A final overriding factor in post-Soviet Russia is its struggle to fend off radical Islam's encroachments in the northern Caucasus. This reli-

gious-political conflict is likewise engulfing the Central Asian republics. It pits Russian troops against Muslim guerrillas in low-intensity
warfare that drains Moscow's resources and threatens the long-term
stability of the Federation. Without a resolution, it is difficult to envi-
sion Russia politically and economically developing into a modern
Western-style state.

Conclusion

At the start of America's 21st century, there are many propositions
bandied about on what Washington's international policy should be.
To be sure, the demise of America's arch foe has set off an ornitholog-
ical metamorphism, where foreign policy doves have become hawks
and vice versa. The Republican Party, for example, formerly champi-
oned bold interventions to confront Soviet moves. President Reagan,
in fact, labeled the USSR an "evil empire" and strove to weaken it by
aiding Poland's Solidarity trade union movement as well as anticom-
munist guerrillas in Central America and in Afghanistan—all the while
robustly rebuilding U.S. defenses. Reagan's successor George Bush
carried on this forward policy. He invaded Panama to capture the
president, a notorious drug trafficker and enemy of democracy. Bush
also assembled an international coalition to expel Iraq from Kuwait in
the Persian Gulf war—the biggest American military operation since
the Vietnam conflict.

   During the Clinton presidency, however, Republicans often pro-
tested military engagements when U.S. vital interests were not threatened. Opponents criticized the Clinton administration for pursuing an
incoherent, even utopian, foreign policy aimed mostly at creating
photo opportunities for the chief executive. They assailed the President
for pursuing an international social welfare system rather than concrete
U.S. interests. Others backed the President's Kosovo air campaign. The
White House pointed with pride to the thaw on the Korean peninsula

and to the toppling of Milosevic in Serbia while expressing alarm at the unexpected unrest in the Middle East.

Clinton and his lieutenants accused Republicans of apostasy from internationalism—the most odious charge that can be hurled at a political opponent since the bankrupt isolationist policy of the 1930s debacle—for their Senate vote against the Comprehensive Test Ban Treaty. The dearth of consensus raises stark questions that will be addressed within the pages of this book—and hopefully by future historians: Was the Cold War victory squandered in the 1990s? Could there have been a grand strategy (or even several coordinated policies) to capture the gains associated with the end of the East-West confrontation? Or, what course of action should the United States pursue in this unprecedented age?

Grand Strategy in the
Post–Cold War World

It is an interesting commentary on the world in which we live that, when I explain the grand strategy course I now co-teach at Yale, about half the people to whom I describe it think I am talking about "grant strategy": how do you go about getting the next federal or foundation grant? This could hardly have happened at any point during the half century that separated the Japanese attack on Pearl Harbor in December 1941, from the final collapse of the Soviet Union in December 1991. Grand strategies then were a fact of life: you did not need to explain what they were or why they were needed. Today they are an endangered species.

Dr. Samuel Johnson provided a reason more than two hundred years ago: "Depend on it, sir, when a man knows he is to be hanged in a fortnight, it concentrates his mind wonderfully." There was plenty to concentrate the American mind in 1940–41, with the result that we had a grand strategy for fighting World War II already in place before we even got into it. Minds concentrated quickly again when the Cold War broke out. By the end of 1947 we had a new grand strategy— containment—to which we adhered for the next four decades, despite confusions generated by our domestic politics, our relations with allies, and at least one grievous miscalculation of fundamental interests, which was the war in Vietnam.[1] We maintained this sense of purpose and direction because we had to. We lived in a dangerous world.

It's not at all obvious, in the absence of the threats posed by Nazi Germany, Imperial Japan, and the Soviet Union, that the United States would have taken on such global responsibilities. We've historically been an isolationist country. It took a lot to override that tradition. But on a single Sunday morning in 1941 it suddenly became clear to all Americans that the security we'd taken for granted throughout most of our history no longer came free.[2] We would henceforth have to work for it, pay for it, and at times die for it. Our interests, therefore, shifted from the regional to the global, our capabilities grew to match them, and grand strategies emerged, out of necessity, for applying those capabilities in pursuit of those interests.

Today we still face dangers, but they are much less clear and certainly not as immediate as the ones we confronted between 1941 and 1991. We have, accordingly, contracted our capabilities, especially in the military sphere, although these still far surpass those of anybody else. But it's not at all apparent that we've contracted our interests: the Cold War habit of leadership is still very much with us. "The success or failure of the American people's foreign policy," Secretary of State Madeleine Albright has grandly proclaimed, "remains the single greatest factor in . . . the future of the world."[3]

---

1. Mark A. Stoler, *Allies and Adversaries: The Joint Chiefs of Staff, the Grand Alliance, and U. S. Strategy in World War II* (Chapel Hill: University of North Carolina Press, 2000), is now the definitive assessment of wartime grand strategy. For containment, see my *Strategies of Containment: A Critical Appraisal of Postwar American National Security Policy* (New York: Oxford University Press, 1982), and a post–Cold War reevaluation in *The United States and the End of the Cold War: Implications, Reconsiderations, Provocations* (New York: Oxford University Press, 1992), especially pp. 18–46.

2. For the nineteenth century concept of "free security," see C. Vann Woodward's classic analysis, "The Age of Reinterpretation," *American Historical Review* 66 (October 1960): 2–13.

3. Madeleine K. Albright, "The Testing of American Foreign Policy," *Foreign Affairs* 77 (November/December 1998): 64.

Perhaps so, but what was the policy? On this point, she and her colleagues in the Clinton administration were less than explicit. There was little need to answer that question during World War II and the Cold War: we were defending democracy and capitalism against totalitarian challenges from both the right and the left. Today, though, democracy and capitalism are hardly at risk. Our culture, our economy, and our principles are more widely emulated now than at any other time in our history. We are more powerful now than we have ever been, but in contrast to what we did during the Cold War, we have yet to answer the question: how are we to use that power? That brings me back to the subject of grand strategy.

I define the term very simply: grand strategy is the calculated relationship of means to large ends. It is about how one uses whatever one has to get to wherever it is one wants to go. Our knowledge of it derives chiefly from the realm of war and statecraft, because the fighting of wars and the management of states have demanded this calculation more than any other documented arena of human activity. But grand strategy need not relate only to war and statecraft: it is potentially applicable to any field of human endeavor in which means are to be deployed in the pursuit of important ends.[4]

Wanted: Generalists

It is striking that during the decade since the Cold War has ended, the term "grand strategy" has hardly been heard. The Bush administration spoke vaguely of a "new world order," but never got around to explaining what that meant. The Clinton administration experimented with terms like "enlargement" and "engagement," but never made it clear what was to be "enlarged" or "engaged." Congress has held no hearings

---

4. The students in our grand strategy course at Yale, for example, have already produced several thoughtful papers linking Sun Tzu, Machiavelli, and Clausewitz to the art of romance, something that is clearly for them, at this stage of their lives, a large end.

on the need for a grand strategy; the media, apart from a few pundits, has mostly ignored it; and the public at large seems uninterested, not just in grand strategy, but in international affairs generally.

Nor have our allies done much better. NATO still looks to the United States to lead it, expressing only occasional alarm at Washington's own lack of clarity as to which direction NATO should now go. The European Union focuses its attention on economic and human rights issues, but hardly at all on how these might connect with international security. Our other allies elsewhere content themselves with regional perspectives, leaving it again to the Americans to determine how each of these might relate to the other, or fit within a global framework.

Indeed, the only places where I hear grand strategy talked about these days are places where things are not going so well: definitely Moscow, to some extent Beijing, and, most interesting, certain corporate boardrooms where the problems of trying to adapt old ways of thinking to new technology are all too real. Dr. Johnson, I think, would not have been surprised to hear that the comfortable and complacent are failing to think in grand strategic terms. For the flip side of his aphorism might well be framed as follows: Depend on it, sir, the prospect of *not* being hanged in a fortnight clouds the mind thoroughly.

As a consequence, the United States has become something rather remarkable: a nation that wields greater power than ever before in its own history, or for that matter in the history of the world, but without any particular purpose. So, should we conclude from this that the need for grand strategy has passed? That the problem of insecurity is no longer with us? That all that need concern us now is getting our grants? I don't think so, for several reasons.

First, even the most cursory familiarity with history would suggest that benign international environments like the present are rare, and that the persistence of unchallenged authority—like that currently enjoyed by the United States—is even rarer. Only the Roman empire functioned under comparable conditions; but given what happened to

Rome anyway, that precedent holds little appeal. Sooner or later even the most powerful hegemon will encounter clear and present dangers. We just can't specify right now what ours will be.

Second, even in the absence of such dangers, a country without a strategy is like a missile without a guidance system. It's likely to dissipate resources ineffectually and spread potential damage far. It can pose as many risks to those who build and maintain it as it does to those at whom it's supposed to be aimed. When the country in question is as powerful as the United States, the problem is magnified. For even if you don't use your power, you run the risk of being regarded, by those who have so much less of it, as a very big giant with a very small brain.

Third, the intellectual discipline of thinking in grand strategic terms is a useful antidote to the specialization that necessarily comes with professional training. There have been instances lately of pilots literally flying their airplanes into the ground—the technical term is "controlled flight into terrain"—because they concentrated too narrowly on some particular cockpit task, while losing sight of their general responsibility to keep the machine in the air until the runway was safely under it. Statecraft, rather like aircraft, requires that those in charge think about a lot of things simultaneously. Grand strategy helps you to do that.

Fourth, organizations are delegating important responsibilities to younger, lower-ranking employees far sooner than once was the case. Business is learning that innovation flows from the bottom up as well as from the top down. International and nongovernmental organizations operate by balancing diverse coalitions just as much as by building firm consensus. These qualities require that subordinates within large organizations know their purposes and be able to decide for themselves how to fit their activities within them—in short, a grand strategic view.

Finally, there's a longer-term reason why grand strategies will be necessary in the decades to come. It is that the authority of government itself, as traditionally understood, is coming under siege from global forces.[5] If democratic principles are to mean anything at all in this new age, there will need to be ways of monitoring these forces—and, if necessary, ways of regulating or even challenging these practices. Governments did just that in the wake of the first industrial revolution: they saved capitalism from its own excesses. They may have to do this again in the wake of the information revolution, and if so, that will really require thinking in grand strategic terms.

It's difficult to try to specify, in advance, what particular grand strategy will be appropriate for various situations. Too much depends on the context—and on the contingencies that are sure to come with it. At the same time, it's not enough simply to make up grand strategy as you go along. You wouldn't attempt basketball, ballet, or bridge without a certain amount of training. And yet, we as a nation invest far more time and effort preparing people for these and other recreations than we do in training grand strategists. The end of the Cold War has produced, not a "missile gap," as the Cold War once did, but a "strategy gap." How might we fill it?

We might start by reviving the respectability of generalists. Grand strategy requires people whose vision is broad enough to take in the entire picture, to break out of the boundaries that separate particular areas of specialization. George C. Marshall, arguably the greatest of American grand strategists, complained frequently about what he called "theateritis": the tendency of certain military commanders to look only at their own needs, and not at the requirements of fighting the war as a whole. A famous Herblock cartoon from the Korean War shows Douglas MacArthur—often a source of Marshall's concerns—planning military operations on a square globe, with only the Asian mainland visible at the top of it. Marshall is reminding him: "We've been using more of a roundish one."[6]

5. For more on this, see John Lewis Gaddis, "Living in Candlestick Park," *Atlantic Monthly* 283 (April 1999): 65–74.

6. Herbert Block, *The Herblock Book* (Boston: Beacon Press, 1952), p. 204.

Indeed Washington was, at the time, which has something to do with why the Korean War did not become the Third World War. But what about our universities, our professional schools, and our think tanks today: are they not geared toward the production of specialists—square-globe people whose limited views are ill-suited to panoramic visions.

There are, for example, the international relations theorists who refuse to look at new Soviet, East European, and Chinese documents on Cold War history because they might mess up the elegance and parsimony of their Cold War models.[7] There are the economists who assure us confidently that an unregulated global marketplace is bound to bring peace, prosperity, and general contentment—even as, in Seattle, they dodged the demonstrators, and smarted from the tear gas. And then there is, most memorably, the NATO briefing team that came to Yale several years ago to make the case for admitting Poland, Hungary, and the Czech Republic. "Might this not anger the Russians, and possibly push them into some form of cooperation with the Chinese?" one of my colleagues asked. "Good God!" the principal briefing officer exclaimed, in front of our entire audience. "We never thought of that!"

How, though, do we reverse this trend toward professionalized parochialism? What should we actually teach a new generation of generalists? I would begin by seeking a set of principles for thinking about grand strategy—principles sufficiently broad to be applicable in circumstances none of us can now foresee. What follows are a few suggestions for what some of them might be, framed with particular reference to the situation the United States faces as it balances the requirements of a new century and administration against the legacies of its Cold War victory.

7. William C. Wohlforth, "A Certain Idea of Science: How International Relations Theory Avoids the New Cold War History," *Journal of Cold War Studies* 1 (spring 1999): 39–60.

First, Specify a Destination

If grand strategy involves getting from where you are to where you want to go, then it's obviously important to *know* where you want to go. Or, to put it another way, you have to define your interests, otherwise your strategy will make no sense. This is what Clausewitz really meant when he wrote the single most influential but also most confusing sentence in the history of grand strategy: that "war is merely the continuation of policy by other means."[8] If I had been his editor, I would have asked him to put it this way: that war is always subordinate to policy, that force must always be used in such a way as to reflect political objectives, that means must be aligned with ends, not the other way around. Based on the rest of what Clausewitz says in his great classic, *On War*, I think he would have agreed.

So what are grand strategic "ends" in the first place? They are both easy and hard to specify, existing as they do in a kind of limbo between the extremes of platitude and profundity. Some are so obvious that it hardly seems necessary to state them: any state, or corporation, or individual seeks first survival, then security, then a reasonably benign environment within which to function. The difficulty comes—and it is here that profundity is required—in deciding what it will take to get these things: what conditions have to be met in order to secure these ends? Defining these is the first great task of any grand strategist, and there are several questions worth asking in going about this task.

First, *is it necessary, in order to ensure survival, security, and a congenial environment, to alter the nature of the system within which you find yourself, or can you work within it?* To put it another way, is your conception of interests unilateral or multilateral? Revolutionaries like Alexander the Great, Napoleon, Lenin, Stalin, and Mao sought to reshape the international system in their own image. They regarded

8. Carl von Clausewitz, *On War*, ed. trans. Michael Howard and Peter Paret (Princeton: Princeton University Press, 1976), p. 87.

the existing order as illegitimate and set themselves about the task of changing it. Their approach was relentlessly unilateral: security for themselves, at the expense of all the rest. The more normal pattern for statecraft, fortunately, has been to construct, perpetuate, or seek to restore multilateral arrangements: security for several, if not for all. Metternich, Castlereagh, Salisbury, Churchill, and the two Roosevelts fall into this category: they were all, in their own way, conservative statesmen, content to work within the systems they had inherited.

A few individuals, like Bismarck, have challenged the status quo at one stage in their career, and defended it at another—but only, in Bismarck's case, after he had redesigned it to suit his specifications. Woodrow Wilson, conversely, sought multilateral objectives through unilateral methods: his vision of a world reformed so as to be safe for both democracy and capitalism was so far ahead of its time that it came across, even to allies and to his own countrymen, as revolutionary and therefore dangerous. As a consequence, Wilson's strategy failed within his lifetime—as Bismarck's did not—because he was never able to decide whether he was trying to work within the system or to overthrow it.

The United States today runs the risk of replicating Wilson's mistake. We have no reason to fear a multilateral world in which several centers of power exist and operate according to a set of common rules: the original objective of containment, after all, was to seek just such a system, and with the end of the Cold War we largely achieved it. Since that time, though, we seem to have switched to unilateral methods in our efforts to sustain it. There's no longer a common enemy to provide a common interest in holding the system together, so we seem to think we've got to do that ourselves by proclaiming our own importance—hardly a sign of self-confidence. We've lost the art of building strategy by consensus; today we do it by instruction, rather in the manner of Woodrow Wilson. And the pupils in the classroom are already getting restless.

That brings up a second issue about ends. Having determined

whether you are seeking to preserve an old system or to create a new one, you must then choose between micro- and macromanagement: *will you need to manage the entire system yourself, or can you set it up in such a way as to delegate much of that authority to the units that operate within it?* Most states have no choice in the matter: they are one of several of roughly equal powers, none of whom has the opportunity to control the system as a whole. But empires, or superpowers (or, to use the currently fashionable word, hegemons), do have a choice: they can concentrate authority or they can delegate it; they can allow autonomy or they can seek to stifle it. It makes quite a difference which choice you make, because a self-regulating system is obviously easier to maintain than one that demands central direction.

Contrast Philip II's management of the Spanish Empire during the sixteenth century, for example, with the way the British handled their empire from the time of Elizabeth I through the end of the nineteenth century.[9] Both empires lasted about as long, but they were hardly the same when it came to efficiency. Or compare the ways in which the Soviet Union and the United States managed their respective spheres of influence during the Cold War. The American system was largely self-regulating, despite the fact that it operated under Washington's protection and according to a set of rules Washington had devised. As a consequence, it proved to be both durable and resilient. The Soviet system allowed far less autonomy, with the result that the states and its peoples were eager to get out, and did so as soon as they feasibly could: Yugoslavia in 1948, China in 1958–59, Eastern Europe in 1989.[10]

It would be a very odd thing if the United States, having won the Cold War, should now begin to adopt the management style of its defeated adversary. That hasn't happened yet, but the increasing com-

9. For an excellent account, see Geoffrey Parker, *The Grand Strategy of Philip II* (New Haven: Yale University Press, 1998).

10. I have elaborated on this comparison in *We Now Know: Rethinking Cold War History* (New York: Oxford University Press, 1997), pp. 188–211.

plaints we hear about American unilateralism ought to give us pause. Things like our apparent contempt for the United Nations, our heavy handedness within international economic institutions, and our refusal to ratify the Comprehensive Test Ban Treaty begin to take their toll.[11] It's one thing to put up with an overbearing hegemon when it's protecting you against something worse. It's quite another when it's the only hegemon in town.

That brings up a third issue with respect to ends, which is that of legitimacy: *what higher purpose does your system serve?* What are its aspirations? What are its values? It's not enough to have a system that exists only to secure the interests of its dominant hegemon, for the capacity of the weak to resist—or even to sabotage—is always present. There has to be some higher purpose, some objective for which all within the system will sacrifice, some common cause above self-interest around which one can build mutual interests.

There's nothing particularly new in this. From Pericles on, statesmen have evoked some set of values—liberty, civilization, salvation, glory, justice, revolution, national or racial or linguistic identity—to gain the support they needed for whatever it was they had decided to do. What's different now, in a democratic age, is that there are so many values to choose from, not all of which are compatible. Can one have, for example, both geopolitical stability and respect for human rights? Both political self-determination and economic integration? Both the prosperity that comes from market capitalism and the social justice that comes from the regulation of market capitalism?

Sir Isaiah Berlin wrote eloquently about the incommensurability of values—about the fact that one cannot possibly have all good things, and that one of the most difficult tasks of statecraft is choosing among

11. Samuel P. Huntington, "The Lonely Superpower," *Foreign Affairs* 78 (March/April 1999): 38, provides a much longer list of recent examples of American unilateralism.

them.[12] Because hope springs eternal, ends are potentially infinite. Means never are. If grand strategy is indeed the calculated relationship of means to large ends, then it seems equally clear that those ends cannot be everything everybody wants: that just as means must be subordinated to ends, ends in turn must be disciplined by available means. But who, among our leaders today, has had the vision to understand the need for such choices, or the courage to make them?

The most useful way to think about this problem of ends is simply to ask yourself: where would you like to be at some specific point in the immediate, intermediate, and distant future? This exercise has the advantage of forcing you to specify not just an ultimate destination but the points you will need to pass along the way. It requires that you consider the vehicle in which you're traveling: will it serve to get you there, or might you need a new one? It makes you think about maintenance, or to put it another way, sustainability. And it demands a sense of direction: knowing the goal is the first and most important step to figuring out how to get there.

Second, Minimize Resistance

There are three great sources of friction, in any grand strategy, that can keep you from getting to where you want to go. They are: what your adversaries do; what you do to yourself; and what the environment in which you're competing does to both of you.

What Adversaries Do

An adversary is someone or some thing that combines hostility with capability. Hostility without capability poses no threat—Albania was very hostile to us throughout most of the Cold War, and yet we didn't

---

12. "The Pursuit of the Ideal," in Isaiah Berlin, *The Proper Study of Mankind: An Anthology of Essays*, ed. Henry Hardy and Roger Hausheer (New York: Farrar, Straus and Giroux, 1998), pp. 1–16.

worry about it very much. Nor does capability without hostility constitute danger: Great Britain, France, and Israel have the capacity today, as nuclear powers, to do us great damage. But they aren't hostile, so we don't worry very much about them. To be an adversary deserving of a grand strategy, both characteristics—hostility and capability—must be present.

You may want nothing more than to live securely in peace; but an adversary can prevent you from doing that. You may want to deny your adversary that right; but he may be able to prevent that too. The adversary, in short, gets in between the ends you have specified and the means available to pursue them.

It follows from this that if you haven't specified ends—if you haven't defined interests—threats have no meaning. The world is full of potential dangers for those paranoid enough to seek them out: they range from the prospect of nuclear war at one end of the spectrum to the possibility of enraged French farmers trashing McDonald's hamburger franchises at the other end. One of the reasons it's a good idea to define interests clearly is that it's a way to protect against paranoia— it narrows the number of threats you've got to confront.

What all of this suggests is the need for a hierarchical ranking of adversaries: for distinguishing between dangers that are clear, present, and potentially harmful, on the one hand, and those that are indistinct, indefinite, and not so threatening, on the other. This requires a cool head and a steady hand, because the most dangerous adversaries may not be the ones that have aroused the greatest anger. That was true of Nazi Germany in World War II: one of Franklin D. Roosevelt's greatest achievements as a strategist was to keep our energies focused on defeating the Germans first, even though it had been the Japanese who actually attacked us.

Or consider the People's Republic of China, with whom we were furious after its intervention in the Korean War. We were wise in the end, though, not to allow our emotions to shape our strategy; for although China was unrelentingly hostile over the next two decades, it lacked the capability the Soviet Union possessed to significantly harm our interests. As a consequence, the Nixon administration was in a position to respond quickly when Chairman Mao suddenly decided, in 1969, that the greater threat to China's security lay in its erstwhile ally the Soviet Union, and not the United States.

Finally, consider a contemporary example. It's not at all clear to me today that Fidel Castro's Cuba stands between us and any vital interest we might seek to pursue. He's hostile, yes, but what is he capable of? Only, as far as I can tell, of making us look foolish by getting so angry about him. If we can today maintain normal diplomatic and economic relations with one of our most persistent former adversaries, the Vietnamese, it's hard to know why we can't keep our cool about Fidel.

What You Do to Yourself

If you haven't defined interests clearly—if you don't know where you're going, if you strike out in several different directions at once, or if you see yourself threatened from several different sources and have made no effort to rank these dangers—then you will surely generate resistance to yourself.

Self-generated resistance can also occur by overextending a perimeter, as Sun Tzu noted some twenty-five hundred years ago: "[When the enemy] prepares in a great many places, those I have to fight in any one place will be few. . . . [W]hen he prepares everywhere he will be weak everywhere."[13] It can happen through underextension—the illusion that it is not necessary to prepare at all, and that the danger will simply go away. It can happen by thinking monodimensionally—by being insensitive to the interests of others, and therefore to the friction their reactions can generate. It can happen by not thinking at all, and hence allowing pressures, not interests, to determine what you do.

13. Sun Tzu, *The Art of War*, trans. Samuel B. Griffith (New York: Oxford University Press, 1963), p. 98.

Grand strategy is an interactive process. A country has to consider the effects of its actions, whether on itself or on others. Or, to paraphrase Pogo, a now obscure American cultural icon from the early years of the Cold War: We have met the enemy, and he or she is us.

What the Environment Does to You

All strategy plays out on a field of some kind, but it is never exactly a level playing field. Circumstances quite independent of what you or your adversary do can cause the playing field to tilt in a way that helps one side and hurts the other. These can be unpredictable events, like weather, disease, famine—or even psychological panic—the kinds of things Clausewitz wrote about when he introduced that useful term "friction" into grand strategy.[14] They can be concealed trends, like the role of the energy crisis in weakening the Soviet Union during the 1970s, or the way in which the information technology revolution strengthened the United States during the 1980s.

The point is simply that you should leverage your assets. It's important to watch the way the playing field is tilting, whether in terms of politics, economics, or culture. You should use those tilts, where you can, to your advantage. You should avoid situations where the tilt is working against you. Or, to put it more elegantly, you should question any strategy that requires you to shovel shit uphill.

Finally, Plan *and* Improvise

Clausewitz made two points about strategic planning that may seem, at first glance, contradictory. It was important, he believed, to plan carefully for war. But it was equally important, when the war came, to be able to throw the plans right out the window, for the real war would never quite resemble the one you had planned for.[15] Precisely because

14. Clausewitz, *On War*, pp. 119–21.
15. Ibid., pp. 139–40.

war is the combined result of what adversaries do to you, what you do
to yourself, and what the environment does to both of you, it is an
inherently unpredictable enterprise requiring a delicate balance between anticipation on the one hand and improvisation on the other.

It's not enough just to make up grand strategy as you go along.
Justice Potter Stewart's famous standard for recognizing pornography—"I'll know it when I see it"—may work in that arena, but not in
this one. The magnitude of what's at stake and the complexity involved
in securing it make advance planning necessary—to say nothing of the
need to overcome, as much as possible, the unpredictabilities of human behavior. At the same time, though, sticking to the plan when
circumstances have changed can be equally dangerous. Proportionality
requires knowing when the strategy is not working as well as when it is,
and that demands a constant testing of plans against the contingencies
they are designed to meet. One way to think about this is to return to
my airplane metaphor.

Pilots, whether operating in a hostile or a benign environment,
value the freedom to improvise. Whether you're flying an F-15 for the
United States Air Force or a 747 for United Airlines, you wouldn't want
to lock yourself into some rigidly prescribed flight plan. You'd want the
flexibility to shift your heading, your altitude, or your speed when you
encounter the unexpected, whether it's a SAM missile or a big bad
thunderstorm or a wayward Cessna. You can never be sure what you're
going to run into along the way, and you need to be able to use your
own judgment—not just that of your autopilot or your air traffic con-
troller—in responding to it.

This is by no means the same thing, though, as operating without
a strategy. For if the pilot hasn't learned ahead of time what to avoid in
flying a plane—errors like forgetting to set the flaps correctly or neglecting to calibrate altimeters and navigation equipment accurately—then
the effects even in a peaceful environment can be as devastating as
encountering an enemy fighter ace in wartime. That's why all pilots,
civilian or military, have checklists: they provide a way, not of *predict-*

ing what is going to happen, but of *preparing* for whatever that might turn out to be.

In a world of indistinct and potential rather than clear and present dangers, perhaps we ought to think of strategy in the same way. We know more or less where we want to go — or at least what we want to hang onto — but unlike the situation throughout most of the Cold War, we have no clear sense of who or what will stand in our way. Maybe what we should do, therefore, is to concentrate on avoiding predictable hazards, leaving room for improvisation to dodge the unpredictable ones as the need arises. We don't need strategic forecasting so much as a strategic checklist — a reminder of known pitfalls for use in navigating around the unknown ones that are certain to lie ahead.[16]

Planning, for Clausewitz, was not a means of predicting the future, but rather a method of preparing for it. He understood that what lies ahead is, for the most part, unknown to us, while what lies behind provides the basis for everything we know. We need theory — what the military would call doctrine — to make that information available to us in a usable form. We need judgment, however, when we relate theory, or doctrine, to practical realities.

Nobody can predict, just yet, in which years over the next decade Yale will beat Harvard. Nobody would doubt, though, that the preparation for these games will be critical: the teams will have to know the rules, they'll have to have the stamina and the skill to compete, they'll have to have the leadership — through the team captains and the coaches — that will get them these things. And yet, nobody would be so foolish as to write out an entire game plan before the game is played: however thorough the preparation, some things have to be left to the judgment of those who actually play the game.

16. I have drawn, in these two paragraphs, from John Lewis Gaddis, "Muddling Through? A Strategic Checklist for the Post-Cold War World," in *Strategic Transformation and Naval Power in the 21st Century*, ed. Pelham G. Boyer and Robert S. Wood (Newport, Rhode Island: Naval War College Press, 1998), p. 126.

Grand strategy demands, then, both the making of plans and the junking of them. Knowing which to do when, though, requires the ability to see all the parts in relation to the whole, for it is only if you know quite clearly where you're going and what stands in the way that you can make wise decisions about which plans to follow and which to abandon. And that brings us back, once again, to the need for generalists.

For grand strategy is, in the final analysis, an *ecological* discipline. It is about the ability to see forests and not just trees, to view the world as round and not square, to relate all of the means at your disposal to the large ends you have in view. It is also, these days, an *endangered* discipline, for in the absence of threats to concentrate our minds there is insufficient incentive to think in these terms. We ought to be capable of reversing this trend without waiting for some new crisis to do it for us; but that will require a rethinking of priorities at the institutions that train our future leaders. We need to make our institutions safe for generalists as well as specialists. We need to train strategic ecologists. The need is great, and the time is nigh.

Meeting the Challenge
of Multilateralism

Identifying the Challenge

It is striking how much of the controversy about U.S. foreign policy since the end of the Cold War has involved disputes about the proper role of international institutional arrangements. These issues have agitated the entire political spectrum resulting in unexpected convergencies between normally antagonistic parties.

Take, for example, the Kosovo intervention by the North Atlantic Treaty Organization in 1999. Both hard-core realists and liberal humanists generally supported the intervention, the former because it indicated a renewed willingness to use force effectively in the service of national interests, and the latter because it put a stop to Slobodan Milosevic's oppression of the Albanian Kosovars.

What becomes apparent is that the relationship to international institutions is now intimately connected with the foreign policy priorities of major states. These institutions remain instruments of states, reflecting their national perceptions and aspirations, and it is best to regard such institutions as neither inherently beneficial nor detrimental. So conceived, neither ideological repudiation nor enthusiasm for international institutions is recommended as a generalized posture. What is proposed as more useful is to evaluate each expression of multilateralism in its specific context, which includes a sense of the global setting, the historical moment, and the ways in which one's own country fits into this larger whole. The speed of adjustment necessitated by the rate and scope of technological change (which is beginning to challenge the character of human existence, as well as to alter our entire understanding of time and space) underscores our need for efficient governance at the international level. For the United States, the policymaking responsibility is particularly great, as its leadership role involves the framing of world order as well as the pursuit of its strategic and moral purposes as the currently most dominant state.

America's new relationship with international institutions can be explored from three perspectives: (1) the institutions of global economic governance (2) a world of regions, and (3) the United Nations System. The three are listed in order of descending priority—so far in this era of globalization, the world economy constitutes the most important multilateral arena.

However, this economistic view overlooks a critical yet unappreciated arena of American foreign policy—our response to the new expressions of regionalism now occurring. Perhaps the most important experiment in world order attempted since the formation of the modern state centuries ago is Europe's current drive toward regional integration. The European Union is a much more dramatic, fundamental, and intrusive challenge to the sovereignty of its member states than the United Nations ever has been. Likewise, in the western hemisphere, Latin American countries are either seeking to join the North American Free Trade Association or forming their own regional groupings that operate without U.S. participation. And in Asia, also, a variety of ambitious regional initiatives are being proposed and are underway.

Finally, the United States' role in the United Nations needs to be reevaluated. This role has been questioned recently both inside the country, where Congress is trying to reduce the U.S. level of financial support, and outside, where countries are complaining about U.S. hegemony. After World War II, and during most of the Cold War, the United States was perceived as the main champion of the United

Nations, reflecting our commitments to social justice, human rights, and the development of international law. The Soviet Union and its bloc were oppressive and secretive societies that regarded the United Nations as "enemy territory." At the start of the Cold War, the United States acted as if it owned the UN, seeking to rely on the organization to reinforce its anti-Soviet stands in the name of preserving international peace and security. But with the decolonization of the 1960s, global priorities shifted to Third World countries, which created tension with the United States, especially on issues of global economic policy and the Arab/Israeli conflict. In the face of such an evolution, the United States became as eager to limit the role and authority of the General Assembly as the Soviet Union earlier had been to prevent unwanted action by the Security Council. Thus ensued an unlikely pairing that had the two superpower rivals jointly advocating the restriction of unwanted UN activities.

The Institutions of Global Economic Governance

Aside from anxiety about a third world war, the greatest concern in 1945 was to avoid the sort of breakdown in the world economy that contributed to the Great Depression in the 1930s. In this spirit, the International Monetary Fund and World Bank were established to provide a measure of international financial stability, especially with respect to exchange rates and liquidity. The effort in this period to include an international trade regime was defeated due to the United States' unwillingness to accept even modest degrees of institutionalized control over private-sector economic activity.

Unlike the UN, the IMF and World Bank operated on the basis of weighted voting that reflected the scale of participating states' financial contribution. From the perspective of U.S. foreign policy, this voting system was seen as beneficial, but it has also caused problems in this era of globalization. It ensured American control, epitomized by locating the headquarters of these institutions in Washington, D.C., as well

as by the World Bank's continued leadership in the person of a prominent, well-connected American. But this degree of Americanization
made these institutions particularly vulnerable to criticism that they
were mere creatures of U.S. foreign economic policy, rather than genuine agents of the organized world community. Third World governments and nongovernmental organizations (NGOs) charged the institutions with having market-oriented, overly interventionist agendas that
mainly benefited local and foreign elites.

With the formation of the World Trade Organization (WTO) in
1995 this pattern of support and opposition deepened. The U.S. Government was the leading sponsor of the negotiations that led to the
WTO's establishment, which disturbed those Americans who are opposed to economic internationalism and globalization. However, the
WTO was backed by most of the political mainstream, who regarded
free trade as the linchpin of world capitalism in the Information Age,
the key to sustaining American prosperity, and highly beneficial to
multinational corporations and banks — many of which were centered
in the United States or its close allies. As a further concession to the
anti-UN climate in the U.S. Congress in the late 1980s, the WTO was
not made part of the UN, being established as organizationally distinct.
(The IMF and World Bank are formally part of the UN system, although they have been operationally autonomous throughout their
existence.)

Critics of globalization have emphasized various objections to the
role of these institutions. The most vigorous objections have been associated with their alleged tendency to favor unsound private-sector
investments and promote policies that neglect impoverished countries
and widen income disparities. These institutions have also been accused of being inattentive to the social and environmental harm
caused by their uncritical focus on maximizing economic growth and
favoring megaprojects. The 1997 Asian Financial Crisis, however, and
its wider reverberations in Japan, Russia, and several important Latin
American countries, shook the confidence of even the most ardent

proponents of a self-regulating world economy. Early reactions included calls for "a new financial architecture" and "globalization with a human face." The IMF's initial response to the crisis was to administer heavy doses of fiscal austerity. Such an approach was widely attacked and held responsible for further jeopardizing the living standards of the poor in many countries. The World Bank was also attacked for giving enthusiastic certifications to Asian economies whose dubious financial practices had contributed to destabilizing forms of currency speculation and collapse of investor confidence. The Bank tended to deflect criticism of its policies by unconvincingly blaming "crony capitalism" for the Asian collapse.

Tangible reforms have not yet followed, although these institutions have taken steps to improve their public relations image, including a proclaimed willingness to listen to the grassroots voices of global civil society. Their leaders have missed few opportunities to affirm their dedication to abolishing poverty and safeguarding the environment, while pledging a renewed commitment to progrowth development and fiscal austerity. The United States' official position in this period of international questioning has been to reaffirm the basic soundness of market-oriented approaches and to resist regulatory proposals for reform, including those that come from Western European governments. American leaders encouraged the view that the Asian failures resulted from corruption and overly dirigiste states rather than reflecting structural defects in the world economy. The international institutions at their operational level went along with this view that the world economy was best off when relying on the efficiency of markets. Wealth disparities were regarded as tolerable in this view so long as it was possible to point to increases in overall material wealth.

In recent years, and especially in the setting and aftermath of the 1999 WTO demonstrations in Seattle, many activists have emphasized the antidemocratic procedures by which global economic policies are formulated, and charged that the neoliberal ideology that guides these policies is insensitive to the well-being of people. Organized labor in the United States was a visible presence in the streets of Seattle, and in protest activity elsewhere, by raising human rights concerns about child labor, poor safety, and low wages in a variety of countries, especially in Asia and Latin America. Territorial concerns over loss of American jobs due to outsourcing and downward wage pressure were strongly expressed. At fundamental issue was whether U.S. policy makers should be more responsive to the well-being of their citizens at home even if it meant sustaining less-efficient economic activities. This call for territorial protection included opposition to policies designed to open national economies to global competition. The American mainstream, with notable bipartisan support, has continued to support globalization despite a growing grassroots resistance. This dominant viewpoint helps explain the Congressional decision to clear China for admission to the WTO despite a variety of well-founded human rights concerns as well as organized opposition from both the left and the right.

When posing the prescriptive question, "How should the United States relate to global economic governance?" it seems evident that there are no simple answers. It would be a dangerous political and economic mistake to pull back from full engagement in the world economy because of territorial pressures. But it would also be a serious mistake to suppose that the regime governing the world economy will be automatically accepted by the citizenry of democratic societies. Such acceptance depends on the world economy being perceived to be both materially beneficial and legitimate by most people. Enhancing the legitimacy of the IMF, World Bank, and the WTO depends on several reforms that can be supported by the U.S. government without altering its embrace of globalization:

- Democratize the operation of these institutions, starting with procedures that assure transparency: all stockholders should be included in decision-making processes, and those corporate and banking interests receiving financial assistance must be held accountable for losses sustained.

- Encourage codes of conduct and voluntary adherence to labor, human rights, and environmental standards as proposed by the UN Secretary General.

- Adopt reforms that generate greater confidence in overseas banking practices, stress anticorruption measures and bankruptcy procedures, and end tax-haven and money-laundering mechanisms.

- Adopt decision-making processes that give greater voice to representatives of governments in the southern hemisphere, including those that are the most economically disadvantaged.

- Examine ways to bridge the traditional ideological divide that pits maximizing economic growth against improving the lot of the economically and socially disadvantaged.

It is certain that foreign economic policy will be a front-burner concern of American foreign policy in the years ahead. The system in place has not yet been tested by serious adversity, although the Asian Financial Crisis provided some sense of what happens when things go bad in a big way. U.S. leaders need to formulate preventive steps in order to ensure that these institutions of global economic governance act as members of a *legitimate* world order. Efforts must include an attempt to counteract globalization's current tendency to reap extraordinary rewards for elites while leaving billions in poverty. This trend is sowing the seeds of future conflict by creating wider and wider disparities between the haves and the have-nots. The pattern also seems to assign future generations the awesome burden of addressing problems that result from presently relying on overly laissez-faire attitudes toward environmental protection.

A World of Regions? A Foreign Policy Calculus

The growth of regionalism in the years since World War II is a complex, and exceedingly uneven, phenomenon that bears significantly on the global role of the United States and the definition of its geostrategic interests.

To begin with, regionalism in Europe, where by far the most ambitious development has occurred, has contributed significantly to American foreign policy—from its formative decades up through the end of the Cold War. European regionalism helped forge American foreign policy goals in at least four respects: (1) it solidified a united front in western Europe that greatly facilitated the policy of containment toward the Soviet Union; (2) it built an institutionalized framework of cooperation among the major European states that made the recurrence of intra-European war unlikely, thereby bringing unprecedented stability to an area that was the setting of both world wars; (3) it offered a partial solution for the problem of Germany and German nationalism—even though this solution initially rested on the East/West rivalry that produced a divided Germany; and (4) it helped with Western Europe's economic reconstruction, thereby exhibiting the relative superiority of capitalism versus socialism, as well as providing markets for U.S. exports and capital.

With the end of the Cold War, the calculus of benefits has shifted somewhat. In general, aside from the former priority of Soviet containment, the same factors are present; however, they are less urgent, and are offset somewhat by a series of new concerns. The most notable of these is that a united and enlarged Europe, encompassing the whole continent and not just the countries in the West, is a potential rival for global leadership. At the very least, now that Europe is no longer dependent on the American Cold War security umbrella, the region is bolder in expressing opposing views on global issues. In the aftermath of the Kosovo War, Europeans talked of creating their own regional military capability that could act without U.S. participation. Even inside NATO there is increasing dissatisfaction with the extent to which American military leaders have dominated the alliance, and it is notable that the KFOR (international security force) commander in Kosovo is a German general. Even during the Cold War, France bristled at the extent of American influence in Europe, and even withdrew from NATO for a time.

Perhaps more relevant is Europe's current relationship to American foreign economic policy. So far, the Euro has not proved a challenge to the dollar in the international currency market, which has decreased European confidence in moving further toward the establishment of a regional polity. European positions on agricultural protection, hybrid foods, intellectual property rights, and cultural issues are often at odds with American views.

On balance, however, the evolution of European regionalism serves American national interests rather well. The fundamental alliance relationship, embodied in NATO, has persisted, and even expanded to include several former Warsaw Pact countries. This suggests that Europe is still committed to linking its security policy to the United States, even at the cost of subordination to Washington. From Washington's perspective, European regionalism is the best assurance of the continent's stability. It is notable that the failure to integrate the South Balkans into the framework of European regionalism partly explains the recent wars in the former Yugoslavia.

Aside from these issues, the larger question for American foreign policy is whether a framework of tightly integrated institutions at the regional level is a beneficial move away from a world of sovereign states. After all, a borderless, prosperous, stable Europe is bound to become a powerful model for other regions in the world, and is already exerting some influence on the shape and depth of multilateral organizations in Asia and Latin America. Each region bears on American interests in its own distinctive fashion. Asia and Latin America tend to regard regionalism as a counterweight to American hegemony—both political and cultural. However, this type of regionalism can also satisfy the important American foreign policy goal of enhancing intraregional security. It can also provide a secular and modernizing alternative to a revival of traditional culture that is likely to adopt an extremist—and anti-Western—form. It would seem, then, that U.S. foreign policy should, at minimum, be respectful toward regional initiatives in various parts of the world, and even encourage and support select movements—such as Africa's attempts to regionalize peacekeeping undertakings.

It would be misleading to view regionalism as a panacea for the resolution of international conflict. It is true that in Europe, membership in the European Union provides benefits, relationships, and identities that downplay the importance of the territorial sovereign state. Possibly, but not assuredly, the sorts of ethnic and religious tensions that have tormented Spain and Northern Ireland for many years might become muted, and eventually disappear, in the setting of "Europe."

In sum, the regional dimension of world politics is gaining in importance as well as altering the manner in which states fulfill their security, economic, and cultural interests. Regional integration also offers non-Western countries a means to insulate their societies somewhat against a feared onslaught of American pop culture that is endemic to globalization. The most appropriate U.S. foreign policy posture is to welcome stabilizing regional undertakings, and to consider responses on a case-by-case basis. In the background is the issue of the character of American global leadership: should it aim for an "imperial" role that views all impulses toward independence and diversity as a threat to its geopolitical designs, or should it lend its support to efforts that bring stability, prosperity, sustainability, and human rights to a larger proportion of humanity? If the latter, then regionalism may be regarded as a generally positive international development whose further evolution is likely to stabilize global affairs politically and economically even if it means a reduction in direct American influence. In an era of economic globalization, such influence is somewhat anachronistic, and far less important than stable management of international relations. A world of regions might become quite an attractive model for the next phase of international relations, a post-Westphalian world order in which the state continued to be the predominant actor, but shared the stage with regional and global economic institutions.

The United Nations: A Crisis of Confidence

Ever since the end of World War I and Woodrow Wilson's call for collective security within an institutional framework of sovereign states, American opinion has swung back and forth on the wisdom of a re-formed world order. At present, due in part to weak leadership from the White House and a unilateralist outlook predominating in the U.S. Congress, there is diminished support for the United Nations. This is unfortunate and casts a shadow across America's leadership of world affairs generally, as well as perpetuates the perception that the United States has abandoned its traditional commitment to making the world more peaceful and equitable. For better and for worse, the UN remains the only truly universal political organization in existence, and provides the peoples of the world with a beacon of hope. The degree to which Washington is perceived as trying to dominate the organization is directly proportionate to a loss of confidence in U.S. global leadership—this in turn leads to charges that America is acting as an irresponsible, "rogue" superpower.

This plight needs to be corrected, but it also needs to be understood. Throughout the Cold War years, the UN's weakness with regard to peace and security was attributed to the Soviet Union's obstructionist behavior. When the Security Council reached consensus on the eve of the Gulf War in 1991, American leaders were optimistic that the UN would now be able to serve consistently as a reliable instrument of U.S. foreign policy. As it happened, the Gulf War, which was mandated by the UN but managed by Washington, elicited charges that the United States was manipulating the organization to suit its will, instead of acting collectively. Two years later, when disaster struck in Somalia, the other problematic side of the U.S./UN relationship emerged. What had started out as a pure humanitarian mission in 1992 was gradually transformed into an attempt to restore governmental authority in Somalia. Factions seeking political control fought back with an attack that resulted in the death of eighteen American soldiers. Suddenly, it became clear that the military prowess so impressively on display in the Gulf War could not perform successfully in the civil unrest and turmoil of a country like Somalia. Several key American leaders and much of the media blamed the UN for the outcome, and spoke against risking American lives in future humanitarian undertakings. The 1992–95 Bosnia War further decreased confidence in the UN, resulting in a corresponding reliance on more conventional statecraft and U.S.-led alliances of like-minded countries—the outcome of which was seen in the 1999 Kosovo air campaign completely conducted under NATO auspices.

Nevertheless, the UN became the main agent of postwar administration in Kosovo. Similarly, in sub-Saharan Africa, the UN remains indispensable in coping with the worst cases of civil violence and chaos that are widespread on the continent. Although with today's global awareness it is impossible to ignore humanitarian catastrophes altogether, the United States does not have to face these challenges alone. Despite its shortcomings, the United Nations is the best framework within which to address such challenges, to the extent that they can be addressed at all.

Thus, it would seem desirable for the United States to adopt a more positive attitude toward the United Nations. Such an attitude could be immediately signaled by paying off its debt to the organization—well in excess of $1 billion for several years now—which has kept the UN on a needlessly short financial leash. It is not in America's interest to allow Jesse Helms to continue to play such an influential role: downgrading and insulting the UN and, at the same time, demanding that its top official come crawling to him in a plea for money.

The new president should build up the American public's confidence in the United Nations. This campaign should emphasize the importance of the UN's role in activities related to human rights, the environment, social issues, and the discussion, generally, of such global challenges as AIDS, fresh water scarcity, and transnational crime and illegal migration. The UN is the best available forum for proposing global reforms and expressing current grievances. Given the degree to which technological innovation, economic activity, and media presence are creating a "one world" awareness, the UN is needed to reconcile territorial citizenship with wider regional and global realities. Instead of perpetuating the UN's image as a plaything of domestic U.S. politics, it is time for American political leaders to better explain why we need a strong UN that can serve our people and others in this era of globalization.

At the same time, it is important not to expect too much from the UN with respect to peacekeeping. Most leading states remain unwilling, by and large, to risk the lives of their citizens for undertakings that do not serve national interests. Even if the United States redefines its interests to include the promotion of democracy and human rights, it is unlikely to fight wars on behalf of humanitarian diplomacy unless its strategic interests also happen to be at stake—as they were to some extent in the Kosovo crises. When genocidal behavior that does not harm national interests occurs, a UN-directed, volunteer initiative may be the only politically viable response.

More elusive challenges involve confronting what might be called "the democratic paradox": the United States government has been championing the democratization of states around the world, while simultaneously opposing the democratization of the UN system. The U.S. government led the opposition to increasing UN sponsorship of the large conferences on global policy issues that were becoming effective vehicles for participation by nongovernmental organizations. These conferences had provided an excellent laboratory for experiments in global democracy. In today's world the practice of democracy can no longer be confined to participation in national elections or the internal operations of the state. There needs to be greater openness to human concerns in global arenas of decision.

One mechanism for overcoming the democratic paradox could be the creation of a global parliament as an additional organ of the United Nations. It may seem to be a utopian idea, but the operation and evolution of the European Parliament suggests that such an institution is both feasible and useful as a means of legitimating governance on a regional scale. The mechanics of establishing a global parliament are complicated, but far from insurmountable. U.S. support for such an institution would restore America's role as a creative and visionary force seeking to improve the international framework.

In essence, the complexity and fragility of the world system in its many dimensions is making a case for increased global governance, and such governance is likely to be most respected if it draws upon the legitimacy of the United Nations.

A Concluding Note

Considering multilateralism from the perspectives of international financial institutions, regionalism, and the UN leads to some rather clear conclusions. First of all, global economic governance is imperative for the continued growth and stability of the world economy, as well as the regulation of new technology. Although the rationale for global governance is widely accepted, increasing its legitimacy here and abroad is one of the crucial challenges facing U.S. leaders today. The absence of transparency, accountability, and grassroots participation arouse criticism and have already produced widespread and diverse opposition to the Bretton Woods institutions and the WTO.

Second, regionalism is responsive not only to the practical realities of economic and environmental cooperation, but also to the affinities of shared historical and cultural experience. The European experience illustrates the momentum that can build up in support of a regional approach, but it also reveals the need to balance integration with national identity. The extension of regionalism to the Western Hemisphere also has intriguing possibilities that should be carefully considered by those who shape American foreign policy in the years ahead.

And finally, the future of the United Nations needs to be treated as a higher foreign policy priority than in the recent past. The organization has been allowed to drift into the doldrums largely because the United States has not lived up to its responsibilities as its most prominent member. There is a need for a strengthened United Nations that acknowledges the rising prominence of civil society actors, as well as the necessity of extending democratic practices to international institutions. So far, the United States' position has exemplified the democratic paradox of favoring democracy at the domestic level but resisting its application at the global level. Creative U.S. leadership in the UN over the next decade depends on gradually overcoming this paradox, and lending support to institutional innovations and procedures of a democratizing character.

Building a World
of Liberal Democracies

At the turn of the century, America stands preeminent in the world, the lone superpower. A decade after the collapse of the Soviet empire, the United States faces no major challengers or threats to its security. By almost any measure of national power and vitality—the economy, the military, the environment, public health, population growth, and the overall capacity of the state—post-Soviet Russia is in steep decline. Its next generation of leaders will emerge in an era "when Russia's past imperial and global status will have become a distant memory."[1] China is a rising power, but its economic and military resources remain vastly inferior to the United States', and for the next two decades at least, it will be no more than a regional power. A Europe increasingly unified within the architecture of the European Union could be a partial counterweight to America's global leadership, but "Europe" is still very far from such capacity for unified action, not to mention the will or vision to lead. And in any case, a Europe unified under the principles and institutions of democracy and freedom represents no threat to American interests. Rather, it will remain a strategic partner, both militarily, within the NATO alliance, and geopolitically, within a dense network of other forms of diplomatic and economic cooperation.

1. Zbigniew Brzezinski, "Living with Russia," *The National Interest* 61 (Fall 2000): 12.

For America in the coming decades, threats to our vital interests —
to our economic and military security, and to our health, well-being,
safety, and integrity as a people — will come not from rival global powers but from regional challengers, rogue states, terrorist movements,
and unconventional dangers. Although militarily no country can rival
us, we face a palpable danger from rogue states and extremist movements that despise the United States for its pluralism, power, and prosperity. No prospect so immediately threatens the large-scale loss of
American lives as a terrorist attack with a nuclear, chemical, or biological weapon of mass destruction. Economically, the single biggest
threat remains the disruption of global oil supplies — but even this
threatens our allies much more than our own country. The greater,
more systemic economic challenge involves implementing new global
institutions to ensure the freer movement of goods, services, and capital
across borders.

The other big threats to American security come from diffuse,
long-term problems that have no leader or capital. These include the
increasing financial power and global reach of organized criminal networks; the spread of deadly infectious diseases such as HIV/AIDS;
global warming and other environmental threats to the atmosphere
and oceans; and the threat that ethnic cleansing in other countries
poses to America's values, integrity, and self-image as a country of many
nations.

In short, the challenges facing American security in the coming
decades are much more diverse and complex than those we experienced during the Cold War, or in previous eras in our history when
America was less globally engaged. They are also less catastrophic than
the prior threat of nuclear annihilation by the Soviet Union.

In this world of diminished but diffused threats, America foreign
policy searches for a unifying rationale. No one logic or priority can
defend and advance American interests in the new century. But as an
overarching mission and purpose, there is no more appealing and compelling goal than the promotion of liberal democracy.

A world composed entirely of liberal democratic states is not a goal likely to be realized in the lifetime of this author, or of any of his contemporary readers. But it is a goal we can proudly declare and strive to advance. And it is not a unilateral imposition of American values. Increasingly, it reflects shared global values. The first great cultural breakthrough came with the "third wave" of global democratization that began in 1974. The regime transitions in Spain and Portugal, and then across Latin America, shattered the myth that democracy was unsuitable for Catholic societies. For half a century, democracy has functioned in Buddhist and Shintoist Japan, and, under great stresses, in Hindu India. More recently it has emerged and taken root in predominantly Confucian Korea and Taiwan, and in Buddhist Thailand. It is now slowly sinking roots not only in the Catholic countries of the former Communist world but also in some where the Eastern Orthodox Church is dominant. Only the Muslim world lacks a clear example of democratic progress or success, and there the goal (if not the practice) of democracy has taken root in Turkey. It also appeals to the bulk of Muslims in Indonesia and to a growing number of Muslim intellectuals and activists in the Arab world, as well as in Iran. As an idea, an aspiration, and a set of values, democracy, with its guarantees of freedom and political choice, is increasingly *universal*.

Why the Global Advance of Liberal Democracy Is an Overarching American Interest

The inadequacy of one single theme to define our national interest is easily demonstrated, for often our national values and interests conflict. A push for the democratization of Saudi Arabia, one of the most repressive and decadent regimes, would serve our values. But it could also displace a friendly regime sensitive to the need for stable oil prices with a hostile Islamic regime that would drive up prices and use the country's staggering wealth to destabilize moderate neighbors. Making human rights or democracy a condition for normal trading relations with China would underscore the value we place on freedom but do nothing to advance its cause in China. Indeed, disrupting China's economic development and global integration would only retard its prospects of political liberalization. It could even provoke a nationalist backlash that would strengthen the most hardline, authoritarian elements.

Nevertheless, an effective global strategy for America in the new century requires an appreciation for how "hard" security and economic interests are inextricably and often subtly linked to the pursuit of liberal internationalist ideals. Throughout this century, and in some respects since its founding, America has seen the promotion of democracy and freedom in other countries not only as part of its unique identity and purpose, but also as crucial to its national security and the protection of its liberty.[2] Now more than ever, as borders become more porous and people, technologies, ideas, and weapons cascade across them, the safety and well-being of Americans—and Europeans, Japanese, and Australians—is bound up with the nature of political order in less-established polities.

It is important to be clear about our goal. It is not simply democracy abroad that will enhance the American national interest. It is the combination of democracy and liberty. *Democracy* is a system in which the principal positions of governmental power are filled and replenished on a regular basis through free, fair, and competitive elections. For elections to be free and fair, and meaningfully competitive, there must be freedom to form political parties, as well as to speak, assemble, organize, and move about during the election campaign. But many electoral democracies in the world are quite abusive of freedom, transparency, and human rights beyond the electoral process. Once a president is elected, he may assume extraordinary executive power with little check on his actions by the legislature or judiciary. Even a govern-

2. Tony Smith, *America's Mission: The United States and the Worldwide Struggle for Democracy in the Twentieth Century* (Princeton: Princeton University Press, 1994).

ment that is freely elected may repress opposition forces, bribe opposition legislators, intimidate and suborn the judiciary, silence dissent, punish independent reporting, shut down autonomous organizations, and countenance brutality by its security forces. Or, liberty may be decimated by the weakness of an elected government: its lack of control over the military and police, its subservience to local oligarchs, feudal elites, or crime bosses, or its loss of control over portions of its own territory to guerilla armies, ethnic rebels, warlords, or drug cartels.

Although the past two decades have seen a remarkable advance of democracy in the world, many of these new democracies are illiberal and function poorly. These afflicted or embattled regimes include a number of the largest, most strategic "swing" states in the developing and post-Communist worlds: Russia, Ukraine, Turkey, Mexico, Brazil, Colombia, Nigeria, Indonesia.[3] In another strategic state, Pakistan, democracy has functioned so poorly and corruptly that it broke down altogether in October 1999. The American national interest lies in promoting not just the electoral form but the liberal substance of democracy.

Liberal democracy entails much more than regular, free, and fair competition for power. In a liberal democracy, elected officials have power as well as authority, and the military and police are subordinate to them. The rule of law is upheld by an independent and respected judiciary. As a result, citizens have political and legal equality, state officials are themselves subject to the law, and individual and group liberties are respected. People are free to organize, demonstrate, publish, petition, and speak their minds. Newspapers and electronic media are free to report, comment, and expose wrongdoing. Minority groups can practice their culture, their faith, and their beliefs without fear of

---

3. For a comprehensive analysis of the distinctive problems with these strategic, unstable states, which could swing in the direction of either a deeper and more stable democracy or a return to authoritarian rule, see Larry Diamond, "Is Pakistan the (Reverse) Wave of the Future?" *Journal of Democracy* 11, no. 3 (July 2000): 91–106.

victimization. Executive power is constrained by other governmental actors. Property rights are protected by law and by the courts. Corruption is punished and deterred by autonomous, effective means of monitoring and enforcement.

While it may be easy in theory to delineate these regime types, it is difficult in practice. In January 2000, Freedom House classified 120 of the world's 192 states as electoral democracies. A somewhat more rigorous count would range from 110 to 115.[4] Whichever number we choose, many of these democracies are illiberal.

We can gain some insight into the value of liberal democracy for America's global interests and security by looking at which countries fall into the various categories of regimes.

Using the definition previously laid forth, there are about seventy-one liberal democracies in the world today. Thirty of these are what I call the "core" countries of the world: the twenty-four countries of Western Europe, the United States, Canada, Australia, New Zealand, Japan, and Israel. Another twenty are "microstates" (mainly island states) of less than one million population, mainly in the Caribbean and South Pacific (and a few in Africa). The other liberal democracies from the developing and post-Communist states form an interesting and revealing list: South Korea and Taiwan; Chile, Uruguay, Costa Rica, Panama, and Jamaica; Poland, Hungary, the Czech Republic, Slovakia, Slovenia, Romania, and the Baltic states; and Botswana, Mauritius, and South Africa. These countries do not generate problems for the United States. For the most part they are our allies, pillars of regional stability and freedom, or at least countries with which we can do business and expect cooperation. They are not the sources of the criminal and terrorist violence that threaten the United States.

---

4. Djibouti, the Kirgiz Republic, Liberia, Niger, and Sierra Leone had levels of coercion and fraud that made their most recent national elections less than free and fair. Other countries, such as Russia, Ukraine, Nigeria, and Indonesia, had national elections sufficiently dubious to put them on the margin of "electoral democracy."

Who *are* the sources of danger and threat for the United States? They emanate from countries that are not liberal, and, for the most part, not democratic. They are the countries in hot pursuit of weapons of mass destruction to aim at the United States: Iran, Iraq, North Korea—all illiberal and highly authoritarian states. They have been the countries where the United States has deployed troops in the past decade to restore order: again, Saddam's Iraq, Noriega's Panama, Milosevic's Yugoslavia, the generals' Haiti, and clan-ridden Somalia. They are the countries that actively support or engage in terrorism against the United States: Syria, Iran, Libya, Sudan, Afghanistan, Pakistan. And they are the countries that house nefarious organized crime networks and drug and smuggling cartels: Russia, China, Burma, Colombia, Mexico, and Nigeria.

The Best Path to Peace

Nothing is more vital to American security than preserving a stable peace. Today there are only four theaters of conflict that could draw the United States into a major and possibly nuclear war: (1) Taiwan, where Chinese Communist leaders could opt for military force in their quest for unification. (2) The Korean peninsula, where war could be engineered by a failing North Korean dictatorship desperate to save itself from political extinction. (3) The Middle East, where a collapse of the peace process might trigger a renewed alliance of authoritarian Arab states against Israel. A Saddam Hussein in possession of nuclear weapons could also resume imperial ambitions. (4) Russia, whose leaders could attempt—via military force—to reinstitute imperial rule over the Baltics and other former Soviet Republics.

None of these scenarios is likely to unfold any time soon. But two facts are striking about this list. First, it is exhaustive. And second, every one of these scenarios owes its potential to the absence of democracy in the aggressor state.

Much debate over the past decade has centered on the "demo-

cratic peace" thesis.[5] Academics exchange verbal ripostes over whether
the War of 1812 or even World War I disproves the argument that no
two democracies ever go to war against one another. Absolute arguments hinge on how loosely one defines the term "democracy." But
one fact is indisputable. *No two liberal democracies have ever gone to
war against one another.* And the intrinsic characteristics of liberal
democracies ensure that they never will. In fact, democracies rarely
even engage in minor skirmishes and are much less likely to let disputes escalate.[6] Authoritarian regimes, on the other hand, are prone to
inciting hostility in order to justify suppression of internal dissent or to
forge a basis of national unity. Thus, there is no more profound and
lasting way to inoculate against the threat of war than to transform
potential aggressor regimes into stable, liberal democracies.

The institutions and norms that restrain liberal democracies from
war with one another also appear to foster peaceful conflict resolution
within their societies. In fact, the resolution of ethnopolitical conflicts
depends heavily on the implementation of equal rights for all citizens.[7]
Representative processes allow minority groups to mobilize and win
representation, whereas the use of violence and terrorism only de-
creases support. It is the system of democracy, and especially liberal
democracy, that offers the best protection for minority rights as well as
the best mechanism for preventing a descent into large-scale ethnic
violence.[8] More liberal democracies will mean fewer instances where

5. This and the subsequent section are elaborated, updated, and adapted from
chapter 1 of my book, *Developing Democracy: Toward Consolidation* (Baltimore: Johns
Hopkins University Press).

6. Bruce Russett, *Grasping the Democratic Peace: Principles for a Post–Cold War
World* (Princeton: Princeton University Press, 1993), p. 119. The statistical evidence is
summarized in table 1.2, p. 21, and table 4.1, p. 79.

7. Ted Robert Gurr, *Minorities at Risk: A Global View of Ethnopolitical Conflicts*
(Washington, D.C.: U.S. Institute of Peace, 1993), p. 137.

8. Larry Diamond and Marc F. Plattner, *Nationalism, Ethnic Conflict, and Democracy* (Baltimore: Johns Hopkins University Press, 1994), pp. xxiii–xxix. See also the
country and regional case studies.

the United States, or the UN (with U.S. funding and military involvement), confront the agonizing choice over whether to intervene militarily to restore ethnic peace.

In fact, more democracies will mean less brutality in general. As Rudolph Rummel has shown in his exhaustive study of deaths from war, genocide, mass murder, and domestic violence in the twentieth century, "Power kills, absolute power kills absolutely."[9] Every instance of mass murder by a state against its own people has happened under authoritarian rule, and the more absolutist the regime the greater the tendency toward democide (genocide and mass murder of innocent civilians).[10] Thus, Rummel concludes, "The way to virtually eliminate genocide and mass murder appears to be through restricting and checking power. This means to *foster democratic freedom.*"[11]

A Socioeconomic Elixir As Well

There are other reasons why the expansion of liberal democracy in the world is overwhelmingly in the American national interest. With their protection of the right to protest and mechanisms of ruler accountability, democracies also do a much better job of protecting the environment.[12] They are also more effective at reducing fertility and thereby lowering population growth, as well as decreasing mortality rates.[13]

Increasingly, statistical analyses suggest that "there is no trade-off

9. Rudolph J. Rummel, "Power, Genocide, and Mass Murder," *Journal of Peace Research* 31, no. 1 (1994): 1.

10. For a summary of the evidence and conclusions, see ibid. The full presentation (and review of the literature) appears in Rummel, *Power Kills: Democracy as a Method of Nonviolence* (New Brunswick, N.J.: Transaction, 1997).

11. Rummel, "Power, Genocide, and Mass Murder," p. 8.

12. Rodger A. Payne, "Freedom and the Environment," *Journal of Democracy* 6, no. 3 (July 1995): 41–55.

13. Adam Przeworski and Fernando Limongi, "Democracy and Development," in *Democracy's Victory and Crisis*, ed. Axel Hadenius (Cambridge: Cambridge University Press, 1997), p. 172; Thomas Zweifel and Patricio Navia, "Democracy, Dictatorship, and Infant Mortality," *Journal of Democracy* 11 (April 2000): 99–114.

between development and democracy," that "democracy need not generate slower growth,"[14] and that in the poorest countries, the level of democracy is positively and significantly correlated with improvements in not only per capita income but in infant survival rates and life expectancy as well.[15] Moreover, as Amartya Sen has shown, "no substantial famine has ever occurred in any independent and democratic country with a relatively free press."[16] In Africa, the only two states that have experienced real success in economic development have been those who have been democratic since independence: Botswana and Mauritius. To the extent that we want to see countries emerge from the chronic poverty that breeds the famines, conflicts, and refugees that haunt our national conscience, democracy provides the best foundation. And to the extent that we want our foreign aid to be effective in promoting economic development, it needs to be conditioned on the institutions of democracy and the rule of law, as I will elaborate below.

Setting Strategic Goals

What should be the strategic aims of American foreign policy in the first decades of the twenty-first century? We can think of these objectives on two levels: one of particular regions and powerful states, and the other of the global system.

The first and most urgent objective must be to prevent the large-

14. Przeworski and Limongi, "Democracy and Development," p. 178.

15. Partha Dasgupta, *An Inquiry into Well-Being and Destitution* (Oxford: Clarendon Press, 1993), pp. 116–21. Bueno de Mesquita and his colleagues explain why democracy provides a favorable institutional setting for development. Political systems with large winning coalitions (typically democracies) require leaders to provide public goods in order to maintain their base of support. In such systems, broadly distributed social spending on education and other public welfare is much higher than in narrow autocracies, whose leaders retain power through the corrupt distribution of private goods to their very small support bases. See *Governing for Prosperity*, ed. Bruce Bueno de Mesquita and Hilton L. Root (New Haven, CT: Yale University Press, 2000).

16. Amartya Sen, "Democracy as a Universal Value," *Journal of Democracy* 10 (July 1999): 7–8.

scale loss of American lives and resources in a war or terrorist incident. This requires a number of steps to improve our military security, including better intelligence gathering, more rapid adoption of the revolution in military technology, and development of a national missile defense system.[17] However, these measures will be ineffectual unless they are complemented by a strategy that attacks the *sources* of threat.

Politically, the most reliable way for the United States to reduce or eliminate the risk of war with a major adversary is by promoting the political liberalization and ultimately democratization of its potential adversaries: China, North Korea, Iraq, Iran. It also requires the transition of Russia from its current half-way state between democracy and authoritarianism into a liberal and fully democratic regime.

There are two political sources of the problems of international terrorism and crime. One is the absence of democracy, or the weakness and decay of democratic institutions, in the countries that breed, harbor, or facilitate these activities. These countries fall into two groups: the dictatorships (Iraq, Iran, Syria, Afghanistan, Pakistan, Sudan, Burma, Cuba, China, North Korea, and some former Soviet states), and the hollow democracies (Colombia, Nigeria, Russia, and certain other post-Soviet states). Our ultimate strategic goal should be to democratize the dictatorships and to give strength and liberal substance to the hollow democracies.

In the latter challenge, however, we face an agonizing dilemma, and this is the second political source of the global criminal threat. Clearly, there is a powerful nexus between the drug trade and the decay of democracy. From Colombia and the entire Andean region, moving south to Brazil and north through the Caribbean to Mexico and even the United States, the drug trade is ravaging the rule of law and cor-

17. The case for transforming the structure and technology of the American military to fully exploit the "revolution in military affairs" is eloquently made by Admiral Bill Owens (with Ed Offley), in *Lifting the Fog of War* (New York: Farrar, Straus, Giroux, 2000).

rupting law enforcement and other democratic institutions. Increasingly, it is becoming a global problem, threatening struggling democracies from Nigeria to southern Africa, and from Turkey to Thailand, as well as numerous post-Communist states. Feeding the insatiable demand for drugs in rich, established democracies—most of all, the United States—the drug traffickers have acquired financial fortunes, intelligence capabilities, and military arsenals that rival the power of Third-World states. However, it is highly doubtful that any combination of measures to combat the trade and strengthen the democracies can solve—or even get a grip on—the problem.

A serious strategy for promoting American security and global order in the coming decades must recognize that the war against international drug trafficking is fundamentally unwinnable. It has no more chance of succeeding than did the ill-fated U.S. attempt to prohibit the manufacture and sale of alcohol early last century. So long as there is a demand for marijuana, cocaine, heroin, and other illegal drugs, there will be ample supply. The sources around the world are simply too numerous, and the financial incentives are too staggering. There are only two ways of beating the drug traffickers and reversing their deeply corrosive accumulation of financial and coercive power. One is by dramatically reducing the demand for drugs, which would drive down prices to very low levels. This can only be done through massive investments in education and rehabilitation. The other way is to legalize drugs and so eliminate the huge profits that the traffickers are able to collect as a result of the illicit nature of the trade. Probably only some sequence or combination of these measures can defeat the drug lords and allow Colombia and other troubled states to establish the rule of law necessary for liberal democracy. Thus, in its emphasis on military countermeasures instead of root causes, the Clinton administration's billion-dollar "Plan Colombia" is tragically flawed.

If we can put the criminal drug traffickers out of business, we will have eliminated the single biggest threat to democracy and order in Latin America. Once their trade expires, so will their ability to fund guerilla armies, corrupt political leaders, and provoke armies and police forces into abusing human rights.

Regional Prescriptions

Even if the drug trade is dismantled, a variety of security threats would remain to be solved. Other types of organized crime are still rampant across the globe, particularly in post-Soviet states, which face the additional burden of establishing legitimate institutions of democracy. Islamist movements, most of them hostile to the West, will continue to mobilize sympathy and support against social injustice and decrepit regimes in the Middle East and Southwest Asia. And Africa will remain a vortex of poverty, disease, conflict, and recurrent humanitarian and political crisis. Each of these regions requires a particular strategy for dealing with the characteristic problems of the region, and a larger, global strategy for fostering democratic change.

While Africa may seem the "hopeless continent," it is also the region where a strategy most clearly suggests itself. The time has long since past (if it ever existed) that we need concern ourselves how particular African states will ally themselves in a global military and ideological struggle. Neither need we worry about the loss of access to strategic minerals, because African states need the money too badly to withhold them from international markets. In Africa, we can and must forge a policy based on principles.

At bottom, Africa's recurrent political and humanitarian crises stem from ruthless, rotten, abusive governance, which must be addressed in order for any solution to succeed. Only by establishing the institutions of democracy and accountability outlined at the beginning of this essay can the economic, social, and political decay of Africa and other countries be reversed. There is no longer any justification for failing to make such reforms our principal strategic goal for Africa.

The challenge in the Middle East is more complicated, because there we do have other interests, as I noted at the beginning of the chapter. But these other interests should not drown out our concern to advance democracy and human rights, for three reasons. First, our values and ideals as a people constitute one of our interests. They cannot trump our military or economic security, but neither can we proceed in complete disregard of our principles without damaging our national identity. Nor can we suspend our commitment to democracy in one part of the world without losing credibility in other regions, and in our more general aim to build a democratic world. That is the second reason. Finally, there is the question of how long autocratic, corrupt, unresponsive but pro-American regimes, of which Egypt is the quintessential example, can stumble on with American subsidies and support before the rot becomes so deep the regime implodes or is overthrown. The Egyptian state is strong enough to survive for some time to come, but the decay is deepening; how can we continue to support a regime that must fall back on increasing doses of repression to survive?

The excuse often proffered for winking at repression in Egypt is that the regime of President Hosni Mubarak supports the Middle East peace process. But it is doubtful whether Egypt really wants to see a comprehensive settlement of the Arab-Israeli conflict. As with Syria, Yassir Arafat's Palestinian Authority, and other Arab regimes, the Egyptian regime is able to justify its political shortcomings and economic failures in the context of the ongoing conflict with Israel. If there is a comprehensive regional peace, this excuse will be gone. Only if the Arab-Israeli conflict is kept simmering can the Egyptian regime and others avoid delivering serious political reform.

After almost twenty years in power, President Mubarak and his political circle confront an increasingly fateful choice. They can either pursue political reform, or continue with the corruption and human rights abuses that are necessary to harness political foes. This is a formula for the eruption of some kind of political crisis, and it is not in the American interest. Not in spite of, *but because of* the vast American stake in a stable and responsible Egypt, we must send a different message. The Mubarak regime should be notified that its $2 billion in annual economic assistance—which has become nothing but a bribe for continued adherence to its peace agreement with Israel—will be reduced each year by 10 percent until the regime embarks on meaningful political reform.

Our particular strategy in the Middle East should be, with help from European allies, supporting liberal forces while rewarding gradual democratizing reforms. With a new, forward-looking king and its history of multiparty elections and cabinet government, Morocco is perhaps in the best position to negotiate such a transition. Morocco, morerover, is one of the countries most in need of incentives the West can offer (such as increased trade and investment, and closer integration with the European Union). Jordan, where another young, Western-educated king has assumed the throne and where multiparty elections have also taken place, may be another. Liberalizing reforms under monarchical authority have occurred in Kuwait and Qatar as well. All of these countries can look to models, in Europe but also in Thailand, of top-down reforms that preserved political order and tradition by transforming an absolute monarchy into a constitutional one. The emergence of even a single successful constitutional democracy in the Arab world would become a powerful inspiration for reform throughout the region, given the growing diffusion of information and the hunger for better government.

The Muslim Dilemma

The Muslim world is in more urgent need of models of democratic progress. Turkey is by far the best candidate for such a model. It is already a democracy, though troubled and illiberal. In its quest for full membership in the European Union it is beginning to address some of its human rights problems, as the internal war in the Kurdish southeast finally winds down. A major strategic priority for the United States must be to assist and press Turkey for market, human rights, fiscal, and political reforms so that the country can finally join the European Union.

There is less we can do with Iran, a strange blend of vigorous electoral competition and stifling theocratic dictatorship where hostility to the United States is still the national line. Nevertheless, pragmatists are gaining political ground. We should reach out to Iran for political dialogue and normal economic and diplomatic relations, while waiting for that moment (which appears increasingly likely to come) when popular disgust with the ayatollahs brings a genuine breakthrough to democracy.

By contrast, in Indonesia, the third crucial Muslim country outside the Arab world, there is much we can do. Indonesia is a classic case of a tentative, emerging democracy where a coherent strategy of assistance might well make a difference. This program must have political, economic, social, diplomatic, and peacekeeping dimensions: political, to strengthen democratic institutions; societal, to empower nongovernmental organizations and build up a culture of human rights; economic, to reform a devastated economy; and diplomatic, to separate the military from politics and to protect the peace in East Timor. Even a comprehensive and well-financed program of engagement will take many years to generate firm foundations for democracy and liberal government. But the stability of all Southeast Asia is at stake, along with the possible emergence of yet another model of a Muslim democracy.

The fourth key Muslim state outside the Middle East is Pakistan, and it is the most troubled of the four. The United States and Europe must press the current military regime in Pakistan to reform the state decay wrought by fiscal disarray, corruption, smuggling, ethnic and sectarian strife, and feudal domination of the countryside. For the moment, these reforms of the economy, social structure, and state take precedence over an immediate return to civilian rule, because "democracy" is unlikely to function without them. The current period of military rule absent severe repression is a window of opportunity that should not be disregarded.

In the predominantly Muslim former Soviet states, the United States must strike a balance between realism and idealism. On the one hand, we need to ensure that Russia does not reimpose a choke hold on the economies on its periphery—in particular the oil flows from countries like Azerbaijan and Kazakhstan. We need to cultivate pragmatic and businesslike relations with these states as well, in order to control terrorism and prevent conflicts that could entangle the United States and Europe. However, we must be wary of joining hands with simply any post-Soviet autocrat unconditionally, for it would undermine efforts to steer Russia on a more liberal course. Particularly within regions, our behavior must manifest some consistency of principle if the assertion of principle is to be effective. This is why we need to press for political reform on Russia's periphery, and invest heavily in those states (such as Georgia) where democratic institutions and practices are struggling to take root.

The Dictatorships

Admittedly, the toughest challenges involve the democratic transformation of long-standing and highly authoritarian or totalitarian regimes with no tradition of democracy: China, Cuba, North Korea, Iraq, Syria. The communist dictatorships in Cuba and North Korea, however, will very likely collapse in the next decade or two, once the countries open up to international trade, social exchange, and information flows, and the people see how their brethren in neighboring democracies live.

However, there are some measures we can resort to for effecting change in these most intractable regimes. The odds are long, but it is increasingly clear what does not work, and what might. What does not work is comprehensive isolation. Sanctions, boycotts, and embargoes can only effectively pressure a regime that is dependent on outside engagement and bereft of any other support. But every rogue state has a patron state (China plays the role for North Korea and Burma, for example), or a set of partners with which it can do business. We must find a different strategy.

Certainly we should not reward rogue states with economic assistance or symbols of honor. But if we cannot fairly quickly bring them down, we must seek to engage them, and, most of all, open up their societies to market forces and flows of information that will gradually undermine authoritarian domination. At the same time, we should support exile groups and offshore radio and TV stations that attempt to open the minds of their peoples and give them uncensored access to news, information, and alternative ideas. This was an important factor in the demise of Soviet-bloc Communism, and it needs to be funded and supported as part of a larger strategy of dealing with closed states. At the same time, the Voice of America must remain a beacon of freedom by doing what we do best: not propagandizing, but giving peoples all over the world, in a vast variety of languages, the news and information with which they can make their own decisions.

China

The biggest and most powerful authoritarian state we must deal with in the coming decades is, of course, China. Even with its declining political legitimacy, its exhausted ideological foundations, and its formidable challenges in completing the transition to a market economy, the Chinese Communist regime remains relatively strong and secure. A strategy that seeks to stimulate that regime's immediate collapse has little prospect of success. But we can lay the foundations for ultimate democratization, and in the meantime promote transition to a more transparent, pluralistic, law-based, and accountable system through several broad means.

First, we need to vigorously encourage China's economic openness and integration into the global market economy. There is growing evidence that by pressing for legal transparency, promoting merit-based hiring practices, and expanding a middle class that is independent of the state, foreign trade and investment are already helping to create the foundations for a more open and liberal system in China.[18]

Second, we need to continue pressuring the Chinese Communist regime to live up to international human rights standards. This requires the same type of multitrack diplomacy that the United States successfully pursued with the Soviet Union under President Ronald Reagan and Secretary of State George Shultz. Under their leadership, principled engagement on human rights proceeded simultaneously, although on different tracks, with economic relations, arms negotiations, and the strengthening of American military power. The Chinese leadership does not like to be embarrassed internationally, but it must know that if it continues to punish dissent and repress religious, cultural, and philosophical freedom, these cruel acts will be exposed and denounced before the world.

Third, the United States should continue to expand a wide range of specific programs that foster the development of democratic institutions and values in China. These programs include training judges and lawyers, supporting pro-reform policy centers in the private sector, helping to translate the work of major advocates of freedom, and strengthening the system for administering competitive village elections.[19] We must learn from our own national history, and that of the Cold War, never to underestimate the power of free-flowing ideas, and

18. Michael A. Santoro, "Global Capitalism and the Road to Chinese Democracy," *Current History* 99 (September 2000): 266.

19. One of the most important elements of intellectual insurgency in China today is the explosion of interest in classical liberal thought. The writings of such classical liberal thinkers as Thomas Jefferson, Alexis de Tocqueville, Karl Popper, Friedrich von Hayek, Milton Friedman, Douglass North, Isaiah Berlin, and Ayn Rand have recently been translated into Chinese. The works of Hayek and the Chicago school economists are particularly hot in China today. Liu Junning, "Classical Liberalism Catches on in China," *Journal of Democracy* 11 (July 2000): 48–57.

the inability of dictatorship to withstand the opening of society to intellectual pluralism.

Two Democratic Communities

The best prospects for democratic progress are in the countries that are already at least formally democratic. There is no greater democratic imperative for the United States than to help consolidate democracy where it is now widespread but unstable—in its own hemisphere. With the opposition victory in Mexico's July 2000 presidential election, the prospect of a community of democratic states—from the North Pole to Tierra del Fuego—is within our reach for the first time. Europe is the only other region that could achieve this goal any time soon, and in most respects it is even further along toward it.

In both Europe and the Americas, several measures are necessary—or at least would be very helpful—to secure democracy throughout the region. First, as is now the case with the European Union and, significantly, with the new "Mercosur" free trade zone among Argentina, Uruguay, Brazil, and Paraguay, there must be a collective incentive structure binding the countries together and explicitly requiring democracy as a form of government. The incentive can be membership in a political community or alliance (such as NATO) but it is even more effective if it has a powerful economic component. The most powerful inducement to the stabilization, deepening, and consolidation of democracy in post-Communist Europe is that it is a condition for entry into the European Union. Nothing would advance democracy in the Americas more than a hemispheric free trade alliance with the same membership requirements.

Second, there must be an explicit mechanism to defend democracy when it is threatened. The OAS adopted the "Santiago Commitment to Democracy" in June 1991, which required immediate consultation if democracy was overthrown. Unfortunately, it left unclear exactly what the OAS should do in this situation. Shortly after it was adopted, the Santiago resolution was put to the test by a military coup in Haiti and an *autogolpe* (executive coup) in Peru. OAS action was ineffectual in Haiti and difficult to discern in Peru. The region needs tougher, more decisive measures to respond to such emergencies.

Third, there must be mechanisms that enable stronger democracies to provide assistance and election monitoring to weaker ones. These measures can deter democratic regression and strengthen democratic institutions.

It is possible to imagine within twenty years that the two core regions of stable, liberal democracy—North America and Western Europe—will expand southward and eastward respectively to take in many more countries. Even if some Latin American (and Caribbean) countries are unable to qualify, a hemispheric community of democracies and open, market economies, linked through free trade, would be a tremendous boon to security and prosperity. For Europe, which is so much further along, the crucial question is, how far east?

The key question for the European community of democracies is whether it will include Russia. The character of the world over the next two decades will be shaped significantly by this question: will Russia gravitate, economically and politically, to the democratic West, or will it fall back on some version of its authoritarian and imperial traditions. As Zbigniew Brzezinski has recently argued, the United States and its European allies, in their ongoing engagement with Russia, should hold open the option of "a truly democratic Russia" becoming closely associated with both the EU and NATO. But at the same time, they should move forward vigorously with expanding the EU and NATO to include, ultimately, all the former communist states of Central Europe. Such a strategy would cement the construction of an enlarged and democratically unified Europe while creating the context for a new, truly post-Soviet generation of Russian leaders to realize "that in order to recover Russia must opt for the West."[20]

20. Brzezinski, "Living with Russia," quoted from pages 14 and 13.

A regional community of democracies is attainable in both Europe and the Americas. But is it now feasible to build a *global* community of democracies as well? We would do well to learn from a conference held in Warsaw in June 2000, with the express aim of establishing such a community. The idea was sound, but the implementation faulty. Participants included not only countries with fragile or seriously flawed democracies, but also several that could only be labeled repressive semidemocracies at best, as well as blatantly authoritarian regimes. For such countries, the conference crafted no means for enforcing (or even monitoring) compliance with democratic commitments. This failing was bluntly exposed when Egypt arrested the entire leadership of one of its most important civil democratic organizations shortly after its delegation left Warsaw.

In the absence of clear monitoring and enforcement, broad inclusion renders democratic commitments hypocritical and disillusioning to the real democrats on the ground in these countries, who come to feel abandoned by the supposedly democratic world. Often, in the course of advancing and defending our interests in the world, we may have to make painful trade-offs that compromise our principles. But the one thing we should not compromise is the truth. Few things can more damage and delegitimize the cause of building a global democratic community than to stand aside in silence or complicity while a dictatorship parades itself as a democracy.

Tactics and Tools for Promoting Democracy

It is beyond the scope of this essay to review in detail the specific tools we have available for promoting democracy.[21] The broad categories are political assistance; economic assistance and incentives; economic and

21. For a comprehensive review, see Diamond, *Promoting Democracy in the 1990s*. For a critical appraisal of political assistance methods and programs, see Thomas Carothers, *Aiding Democracy Abroad: The Learning Curve* (Washington, D.C.: The Carnegie Endowment for International Peace, 1999).

political engagement; conditionality for aid, debt relief, and entry into regional unions; diplomatic pressure; and military intervention.

Military intervention and occupation is not a realistic or promising method to advance liberal democracy in the world, despite the historically specific cases of Germany and Japan after World War II. But we must make more vigorous and coherent use of the other means at our disposal. One of the most important developments in the post–Cold War world has been the emergence of a stream of professional specialists within the U.S. Agency for International Development (USAID) who focus on political assistance programs to help develop the institutions of democracy. Through USAID, the National Endowment for Democracy (NED), and other programs, the United States now spends roughly $700–800 million annually in the provision of such democratic assistance. Although this sounds like a lot of money, it is less than 10 percent of our total aid budget, and it leaves chronic needs unmet and worthy proposals unfunded when one considers the scale of the challenges throughout the developing and post-Communist worlds. Political development assistance must also be able to respond quickly to emergencies and new opportunities, as in Indonesia in the wake of the transition from the Suharto dictatorship. This suggests the need for a substantial fund (perhaps $100 million) that is not tied to a particular country or region and can be dispensed as the need arises. The current level of funding for NED, which is only a little more than $30 million annually, should also be substantially increased.

In fact, our entire approach to aid needs to be rethought. We view it in part as a charitable act, a measure of our generosity as a nation. But it is not charitable to indulge and sustain wasteful, corrupt, abusive governance. Nor will anything be gained for human development by unconditionally relieving the debts of poor countries, as a growing chorus of private groups and European governments are calling for. For the poorest nations of Africa and other parts of the developing world, there needs to be a new bargain: debt relief for democracy and development for good governance. Relief of debt and official economic assistance (other than emergency humanitarian aid) must be conditioned on freedom of the press, freedom of association, judicial independence, electoral accountability, and independent institutions to audit government accounts and monitor and punish corruption. Conditionality must lock countries into these institutions of good governance, instead of offering a one-time reward for political concessions that can be withdrawn upon receipt of the check. Instead of canceling the debt of qualifying countries, the United States—along with other creditor states and multilateral banks—should suspend debt repayment for qualifying countries and then retire the debt at 10 percent a year for every year the state adheres to the above political conditions.

It is not enough to require countries to meet these conditions as they receive aid. This has led to a hopeless cat-and-mouse game with problematic governments like that of Daniel arap Moi in Kenya. The real obstacle to development is not the debt itself but "the lack of political incentives to inhibit leadership from squandering the nation's economic resources."[22] These incentives are generated by democracy, an open society, and a rule of law. Effective conditionality therefore requires that states substantially meet the conditions, with binding and credible institutional reforms, in advance of any debt relief and as a requirement for any continued aid. Many regimes will have to change the entire way they govern in order to qualify.

In short, America must reinvent its foreign aid policy around a "tough love" approach that demands results and puts forward political and economic freedom as the indispensable foundation of human development.

---

22. Bruce Bueno de Mesquita and Hilton L. Root, "Improving the Effectiveness of Donor-Assisted Development," in Governing for Prosperity, ed. Bueno de Mesquita and Root, p. 235.

What Prospect?

If we focus too simplistically on the tough, intractable cases of resiliently authoritarian states, or of autocratic states that are collapsing altogether, the prospects for building a much more democratic world may appear dim. Certainly, the challenges are daunting, and a number of strategic states—from Russia and Ukraine to Mexico, Brazil, South Africa, Nigeria, and Indonesia—are perched more or less precariously on the margins of democracy, liable to swing either way in the years ahead. They require clear, innovative, and focused strategies of pressure and support to pull them gradually into the orbit of stable, liberal democracies. Other regimes, such as communist China, require a longer-term strategy for plowing the social, cultural, and economic soil of political change.

It is far from a hopeless task. No time in history has witnessed more rapid and widespread global progress of freedom and democracy than the last generation. There are many challengers, but there is no broadly appealing opposition ideology. Even many Islamist forces are searching for a way to reconcile a devout commitment to Islam with the pluralism and freedom of democracy. Increasingly, commitment is gathering across regions and cultures not just to human rights in their separate dimensions but to democracy as a *system of government* that best guarantees all other human rights, including fundamental human dignity.

In short, never in world history has there been a more fertile and propitious moment for wedding the founding principles of America to its global strategy and power. It is now possible to imagine a world in which all the major component states will be liberal democracies. It is now time to declare this our goal as a country, and to turn our resources, our energy, our imagination, and our moral and political leadership in the world toward that end.

Globalization and
U.S. International Economic Policy

Political opposition to "globalization" has grown rapidly during the last few years. Protesters in Seattle, Washington D.C., Prague, and other cities have rallied against the alleged evils of an increasingly interconnected world economy—the so-called "Washington Consensus." Activists have argued that the *internationalization* of the world economy has resulted in a number of ills. In particular, they have argued that freer trade—both in goods and in financial claims has had a negative effect on poorer countries. Globalization has increased poverty, heightened inequality and cultural dislocation, and even contributed to the degradation of the environment, they say. Moreover, according to these critics, internationalization has not generated higher economic growth, as predicted by economic theory.

The main objective of the recent wave of protests is to influence public policy—especially with regard to international trade and capital mobility (see Wallach 2000).

But much of the current debate on globalization is based on anecdotes, and has lacked a serious evaluation of the empirical and historical evidence. Although the international financial crises of the 1990s—in Mexico, East Asia, Russia, and Brazil—did provide material fuel to opponents of free trade, it appears that this campaign against economic internationalism has begun to pay off, and to have an effect in influential circles, including U.S. policy. For example, Joe Stiglitz, the former Chairman of the U.S. Council of Economic advisors, has recently argued that emerging markets should restrict the mobility of capital. More importantly, and partially based on the notion that globalization hurts the poor, the United States Congress recently denied President Clinton "fast track" authority to negotiate free-trade agreements.

Any serious analysis of the effects of international openness on social conditions has to start by recognizing that faster economic growth is the most effective way to reduce poverty. Under most conditions, faster growth results in employment creation, and contributes to an increase in wages. In that regard then, rapid economic growth is a necessary—although not always a sufficient—condition for improved social circumstances. This important point is frequently ignored by the internationalization critics.

The purpose of this chapter is to deal with the connection between economic openness and economic performance. I wish to make two points: first, that currently popular "anti-internationalization" views are *not* supported by the existing body of scholarly work on the effects of free trade. Second, that the future of free trade in the world will largely depend on U.S. policy on the subject. The unmistakable conclusion from this discussion is that as we firmly enter the twenty-first century the United States should continue to be the driving force behind free trade. The chapter is organized as follows: the first section is devoted to discussing the effects of freer trade on economic performance. The analysis focuses on economic growth and productivity, and reviews the existing cross-country comparative and historical evidence. The next section deals with the more controversial issue of capital mobility and economic performance. The last section contains conclusions and a discussion of existing evidence on the relationship between openness and income distribution.

Trade Openness and Economic Performance:
The International Evidence

For more than a century, social analysts have debated the connection between trade policy and economic performance. According to liberal economists, freer trade results in faster growth. On the other side, however, are those who argue that protectionism helps economic performance. This controversy continues in today's period of unprecedented trade liberalization, despite numerous empirical studies that appear to show openness positively affects growth. The most prominent trade liberalization skeptics include Princeton University's Paul Krugman and Harvard University's Dani Rodrik, who have argued that the effect of openness on growth is, at best, very tenuous, and at worst, doubtful.[1] Two issues have been at the core of these controversies: First, until recently, economic theory had difficulty linking trade policy to faster sustained growth. And second, the empirically oriented scholarly literature on the subject has been affected by serious data problems. During the last decade, however, there has been tremendous progress in both of these areas.

Theoretical Issues

The so-called new theories of growth have provided persuasive evidence that openness benefits growth. Mathematical models developed by Stanford University's Paul Romer and University of Chicago Nobel laureate Robert Lucas, have shown that countries with more economic openness are ideally poised to take advantage of greater "economies of scale." This, in turn, heightens productivity and speeds up economic growth.

At the core of this economic model is the belief that greater openness helps poor countries accelerate the rate of technological innova-

---

1. See Krugman (1995), Fernadez and Rodrik (2000), and the survey by Edwards (2000).

tion — an insight first advanced in the nineteenth century by classical political economist John Stuart Mill. In the 1950s, this idea was reincarnated in the "learning by looking" principle of Nobel laureate W. Arthur Lewis. According to his theory, openness allows poorer nations to learn from more advanced ones. Models in the "new theory of growth" tradition have showed that a higher degree of openness encourages a "catching-up" process, allowing poorer countries to close the gap between them and wealthier nations. By the end of the 1990s, most economists accepted the theoretical notion that openness usually improves economic performance. Whether this theoretical possibility is indeed supported by reality is, of course, a matter for empirical and historical work.

The Empirical Evidence

One of the most serious difficulties in compiling such empirical evidence has been finding internationally comparative measures of trade policy orientation. For example, while some characterize South Korea as having an open and outward-oriented economy, others use it as a prime example of a semiclosed economy impeded by government intervention.[2]

For a long time, this lack of high quality, internationally comparative data made it difficult to use advanced statistical models to assess conclusively whether, as the new theories suggest, more-open countries have indeed out performed nations that restrict international trade. This state of affairs, however, has changed in the last few years, as new trade orientation indexes have been computed, and as many academics have made a concerted effort to generate results that are not affected by the trade orientation index.

Some economists have tried to tackle these problems by classifying countries according to the degree to which trade is distorted. The Heritage Foundation index of trade policy — which classifies countries into

---

2. See Edwards (1993) for a detailed discussion.

five categories according to the level of tariffs and other (perceived) distortions—is a good recent example of this approach.[3] This type of index had been started with the World Bank's 1987 *World Development Report*, where an "outward orientation" index for forty-one countries at two points in time was constructed. The classification of Korea as a "strongly outward-oriented" country in both the 1963–73 and 1973–85 periods elicited some controversy, however, because it has been argued that the Korean trade regime was considerably more restrictive in the former period. In a 1991 World Bank project, directed by Hebrew University professor Michael Michaely, experts constructed a "subjective index" of trade liberalization for nineteen countries in order to track the evolution of trade policy through time. A serious limitation of these efforts, however, was that these indexes were not comparable across countries, and thus could not help answer questions about the effects of open economies.

In the second half of the 1990s, scholars stepped up the effort to understand the relationship between trade policy and economic performance. An important step was taken by Harvard's Jeffrey Sachs and Andrew Warner, who used a number of alternative trade-related indicators to construct a composite openness index for more than one hundred countries. The indicators included, among other things, import tariffs, social organization, and black-market premiums in the foreign exchange market.

This indicator constituted a significant improvement over previous attempts. It allowed the authors to control for other growth determinants and show that countries with an open-trade regime clearly out performed those that were closed. This study has become extremely influential, and has added significantly to clarifying empirical uncertainties.

In 1998, I wrote an article that explored the way trade policy affects

3. Krueger (1978) is an early attempt to use dummy variables to classify trade regimes.

the growth of productivity across countries. In this article I made a particular effort to deal with the measurement issues that had affected previous literature. Using data from ninety-three countries, I compared nine different indexes of trade policy, in an effort to determine whether productivity growth is faster in more-open economies. If, I argued, the same broad conclusion was achieved with each of these nine indicators, we could surmise a positive relationship between trade policy and economic performance. The results did indeed support this hypothesis, and suggested very strongly that more-open countries have experienced faster productivity growth.

In 1999, Jeffrey Frankel and David Romer, from the University of California at Berkeley, presented new results on the relationship between trade policy and economic growth. This important and increasingly influential paper addressed a number of statistical and technical issues that had hampered previous efforts. It provided substantial evidence in support of the hypothesis that trade openness plays a major role in explaining cross-country differentials in economic performance.

To summarize, while activists and the media have relied almost exclusively on stories and anecdotes, scholars have been seriously engaged in trying to provide scientific evidence on the relationship between trade orientation and growth. These efforts have focused on two aspects of the problem: (1) developing coherent and solid theoretical (mathematical) models on the effects of openness on performance; and (2) using convincing internationally comparative indexes of trade policy orientation. These efforts have produced a body of work that has collectively shown, quite conclusively, that more-open countries perform better—in terms of productivity and GDP growth—than countries that pursue protectionist policies. To the extent that policy makers worry about the economic performance of the world economy, there is no doubt they should pursue further trade liberalization. And there is little doubt, furthermore, that, in order for this type of policy to be effective, it has to be supported by the leading countries, and especially the United States.

Freedom of Capital Mobility and Economic Performance

The opening of domestic capital markets to foreigners is, perhaps, the most reviled aspect of the so-called Washington Consensus. In opposing more capital flow between countries, the antiglobalization activists are not alone. Indeed, a number of academics have argued that the free flow of private capital during the 1990s is what caused that decade's financial crises. According to this view, increased capital mobility inflicts many costs and generates limited benefits to emerging nations. And because these countries lack modern financial institutions, they are particularly vulnerable to the volatility of global financial markets, the argument goes. This vulnerability, it is posited, will be higher in countries with a more-open capital account. Moreover, many globalization skeptics have argued that there is no evidence supporting the view that a higher degree of capital mobility has a positive impact on economic growth in the emerging economies (Rodrik 1998).

The opposition to an increased degree of capital mobility has been characterized by a very limited number of empirical analyses. In this section I review the evidence on the relationship between economic performance and capital mobility in the world economy. I am particularly interested in understanding two related issues: first, is there any evidence at the global level that greater capital mobility is associated with higher growth? And second, is the relationship between capital mobility and growth different for emerging and advanced countries? First, I will review the cross-country evidence on the subject. Then I will turn to recent experiences with controls on capital inflows. I argue that the merits of these types of controls have been greatly exaggerated in recent policy debates.

Theoretical Background

According to economic theory, countries with fewer market constraints will tend to perform better than countries with constraints and regulations that impede market functions. As pointed out in the preceding section, during the last few years most (but not all) economists have come to agree that freer trade in goods and services results in faster economic growth. In standard theoretical models this "free trade" principle extends to the securities trade—countries with fewer restrictions on capital flow tend to out perform isolationist countries. This view is clearly expressed by Harvard's Ken Rogoff in his 1999 essay in the *Journal of Economic Perspectives.*

But whether the gains of free-flowing capital are as large as Ken Rogoff believes is largely an empirical question. In the rest of this section I critically discuss the existing evidence on the subject.

Capital Mobility and Economic Performance: Comparative Evidence

During most of the last fifty years, the vast majority of what we today call emerging nations severely controlled international capital movements. This was done through a variety of means, including taxes, administrative restrictions, and outright prohibitions. It has only been in the last decade or so that serious consideration has been given to increasing capital flow in less-advanced nations. Many analysts have associated these proposals to free capital mobility with the policy dictates of the so-called Washington Consensus.

The inherent difficulty in measuring how free a country's capital flow is occupies the center of the debate. Earlier studies compared the private rates of return across countries. In 1980, Feldstein and Horioka used savings and investment ratios to determine the "true" degree of countries' capital mobility.

More recently, scholars have used information contained in the International Monetary Fund's *Exchange Rate and Monetary Restric-*

tions. This indicator has been recently used by Rodrik (1998) to investigate the effects of capital controls on growth, inflation, and investment between 1979 and 1989. His results suggest that, after controlling for other variables, capital restrictions have no significant effects on macroeconomic performance. This study has become quite influential, and is often used by internationalization skeptics to argue that, indeed, greater capital mobility has not improved performance. However, these IMF-based indexes have serious shortcomings due to their generality and failure to distinguish between different degrees of capital restrictions. Moreover, such indexes fail to distinguish between the types of flow being restricted, and they ignore the fact that, as discussed above, legal restrictions are frequently circumvented. For example, according to Rodrik's IMF-based indicator, Chile, Mexico, and Brazil were subject to the same degree of capital controls during 1992–94. In reality, however, the three cases were extremely different. While in Chile there were restrictions on short-term inflows, Mexico had (for all practical purposes) free capital mobility, and Brazil had in place an arcane array of restrictions.

Paradoxically, perhaps, it has been a political scientist, rather than an economist, that has made the greatest progress in measuring capital mobility. Dennis Quinn from Georgetown University has constructed the most comprehensive set of cross-country indicators to measure capital flow. His indicators cover twenty advanced countries and forty-five emerging economies. These indexes have two distinct advantages over other indicators: First, they are not restricted to an "either/or" classification that labels capital accounts as either open or closed, with no in-between. Instead, Quinn grades countries on a 0 to 4 scale, with 4 signifying a very open capital account. Second, Quinn's indexes cover more than one time period, allowing researchers to investigate whether there is a connection between capital account *liberalization* and economic performance. This is, indeed, a significant improvement over traditional indexes that have concentrated on a particular period in time, without allowing researchers to analyze whether open countries' performance has changed. Quinn's empirical results provide some support for the theory that countries with more capital flow perform better than countries with restrictions.

One of the most important policy questions—and one that is at the heart of recent debates on globalization—is whether globalization produces the same economic results in similar advanced and emerging economies. In fact, according to many intellectually prominent globalization skeptics, capital account liberalization is not bad, per se. The problem, in their view, is that the emerging countries are unprepared for it. This is because the poorer nations do not have the institutions necessary to efficiently handle large movements of capital. Using a statistical model, I recently investigated the above convention, as well as whether higher-capital mobility increases growth. I relied on Quinn's indicator of capital openness, and on precisely compiled productivity growth data. My results suggest, quite strongly, that how open-capital accounts effect economic performance depends on the development level of the country in question. Underdeveloped countries lack the institutional framework to reap the benefits of an integrated market. This suggests that the sequencing of reform matters. Before opening the capital account, countries should reform their domestic capital markets, putting in place a modern, efficient and dynamic supervisory system.

Controls on Capital Inflows: How Effective?

Some scholars, including Joe Stiglitz, former chair of the U.S. Council of Economic Advisors, have argued that multilateral institutions— namely the IMF and the World Bank—should promote controls on capital inflows in developing countries. Much of the enthusiasm for this is based on Chile's experience with this type of policy during the 1990s. In fact, Stiglitz has said, "You want to look for policies that discourage hot money but facilitate the flow of long-term loans, and there is evidence that the Chilean approach or some version of it, does this." Chile's system of capital controls was in operation from 1991 to

1998, and was based on a zero-interest deposit in the Central Bank that pertained to 30 percent of its capital inflows. This deposit had a maturity of one year, and was equivalent to a tax on capital inflows.

Chilean economists Jose De Gregorio, Rodrigo Valdes, and myself have studied the effects of Chile's capital controls in great detail.[4] Our conclusions are that the effectiveness of Chile-style controls has been overestimated. Our analysis suggests that the controls helped Chile's economic growth only in the short term and at a quantitatively insignificant level. But the evidence does suggest that Chile was vulnerable to the vicissitudes of other emerging markets. Thus, my view is that although Chile-style controls may be useful in the short run, and as part of a transitional liberalization strategy, it is important not to overemphasize their merits.

There are many dangers associated with capital controls. First, they increase the cost of capital, especially for small and midsize firms. Second, there is always the temptation to transform these controls into a permanent policy. And third, there is a danger that policy makers and analysts will become overconfident, neglecting other key aspects of economic policy. This indeed, helped contribute to the Korean financial crisis. Until quite late in 1997, international analysts and local policy makers believed that, due to the existence of restrictions on capital mobility, Korea was largely immune to a currency crisis. So much so that, after giving the Korean banks next-to-worst ratings, Goldman-Sachs argued that Korea's "relatively closed capital account" offset these indicators. As a consequence, during most of 1997 Goldman-Sachs downplayed the extent of Korea's problems. If, however, the firm had recognized that capital restrictions cannot truly protect an economy from financial weaknesses, Goldman-Sachs would have clearly anticipated the Korean debacle, as it anticipated the Thai meltdown.

---

4. Other scholars have also looked at this issue. See my 1999 article for the references.

Conclusions

In this chapter I have discussed the effects of economic openness on economic performance. I have argued that recent demonstrations on the evils of globalization have largely ignored the existing scholarly evidence on the subject. The results reported in this paper indicate, quite conclusively, that countries that are more open to international trade tend to outperform protectionist countries. With respect to international capital mobility, the existing evidence suggests that a greater degree of openness may have a positive effect on economic performance. Whether this indeed occurs depends on the degree of development of a country's domestic capital market. This suggests that countries should implement an efficient financial sector supervisory system before opening the capital account fully. The combination of these two policies will have important positive effects on performance.

The importance of these results cannot be underestimated. There is overwhelming evidence that faster economic growth is the most important channel for reducing poverty and improving social conditions. This means, then, that any effort to reduce the extent of poverty in the world should emphasize greater openness throughout the world. This quest for increased international liberalization should, in fact, be one of the most important—if not the most important—element of the U.S. policy toward global prosperity.

References

De Gregorio, Jose, Rodrigo Valdes, and Sebastian Edwards. (2000). "Controls on Capital Inflows. Do They Work?" *Journal of Development Economics* 63 (1): 59–83.

Dollar, David, and Aart Kraay. (2000). "Growth Is Good for the Poor." World Bank, World Development Research Group, mimeo.

Edwards, Sebastian. (1993). "Openness, Trade Liberalization and Growth in Developing Countries." *Journal of Economic Literature* 31 (3): 1358–93.

Edwards, Sebastian. (1998). "Openness, Productivity and Growth: What Do We Really Know?" *Economic Journal* 180 (447): 383–98.

Edwards, Sebastian. (1999). "How Effective Are Capital Controls?" *Journal of Economic Perspectives* 13 (4): 65–84.

Edwards, Sebastian. (2000). "Capital Flows and Economic Performace: Are Emerging Economies Different?" Presented at the Kiel Conference.

Feldstein, Martin, and Charles Horioka. (1980). "Domestic Saving and International Capital Flows." *Economic Journal* 90 (June): 314–29.

Fernandez, Rafael, and Dani Rodrik. (2000). "Trade and Growth: A Skeptic's Perspective." *NBER Macroeconomic Annual.*

Frankel, Jeffrey, and David Romer. (1999). "Does Trade Cause Growth?" *American Economic Review* 89 (3): 379–99.

Krueger, Anne. (1978). *Foreign Trade Regimes and Economic Development.* Cambridge: Ballinger.

Krugman, Paul. (1995). "The Myth of Asia's Miracle." *Foreign Affairs* 73 (6): 62–78.

Quinn, Dennis. (1997). "Correlates of Changes in International Financial Regulation." *American Political Science Review* 91, 3: 531–51.

Rodrik, Dani. (1995). "Trade Policy and Industrial Policy Reform." In Jere Behrman and T. N. Srinivasan (eds.), *Handbook of Development Economics*, Vol. 3B. Amsterdam: North Holland.

Rodrik, Dani. (1998). "Who Needs Capital-Account Convertibility?" in *Should the IMF Pursue Capital-Account Convertibility*, Essays in International Finance No. 207. Princeton: Princeton University Press.

Rogoff, Keneth. (1999). "International Institutions for Reducing Global Financial Instability." *Journal of Economic Perspectives* 13 (4): 21–42.

Sachs, Jeffrey, and Andrew Warner. (1995). "Economic Reform and the Process of Global Integration." *Brookings Papers on Economic Activity* 1: 1–118.

Szelekey, Miguel. (2000). "Income Distribution and Reform." Inter-American Development Bank, mimeo.

Wallach, Lori. (2000). "Why Is This Woman Smiling? An Interview with Lori Wallach." *Foreign Policy* 118 (spring): 13–17.

National Interests and
Measured Global Activism

Poised on the cusp of a new millennium, American power and influence in world affairs have never stood so resplendent. Since the demise of the Soviet Union a decade ago, the United States stands unchallenged by a single state or any foreseeable league of states. Its powerhouse economy, unrivaled military forces, technological prowess, and even its popular cultural sway all bear testament to America's ascendancy. Great prosperity at home and peace abroad enshrine the current period as a golden epoch in the nation's history.

This preponderance of power has, in fact, perplexed politicians, pundits, and academicians as to what international course the United States should sail. At the dawn of the 21st century, the United States confronts a radically altered international landscape with neither a clear goal nor a compass for foreign affairs. Lacking a superpower rival for the last decade, the United States has had trouble defining an international role.

This chapter assesses the United States' struggle to meld a post–Cold War foreign policy, region by region, crisis by crisis. The chapter then concludes by taking account of the various approaches tried—their goals and their pitfalls—and lays out a case for measured global activism. There is no other realistic option than an internationalist role for the United States. Such advocacy is cognizant of America's historical role and its future interests. Withdrawal or even "realist" prescriptions designed to reject moral guidelines in favor of a self-interests-only foreign policy will not guarantee American interests. During the 1920s and 1930s, the United States slid into isolationism to avoid world problems and paid a heavy price when it belatedly had to confront militarized and expansionist states in World War II. America has a vested interest in peaceful change and broadly shared prosperity overseas. A major European or Asian war at the least would impact America's well-being and at worst would draw the United States into the conflict.

The United States ought to help alleviate natural and man-made calamities in far-off lands. International passivity is no virtue in a world where weapons proliferation, international terrorism, and geostrategic realignments are afoot. But our foreign policy must not become a prisoner to the Haitis and Somalias of the world. Action ought to be undertaken only when costs can be kept in check. And, just as in wars, coalition intervention should be embraced, as much as to share burdens as to deflect charges of American hegemony.

For over a hundred years, influential Americans have believed that the road to world peace could be paved with economic development, commercial integration, and international treaties. Before and after World War I, American policy makers and many public intellectuals gave voice to this vision. In the 1920s, this idealism led to the League of Nations, an arms control agreement to limit the size and number of warships, and even a treaty—the Kellogg-Briand Pact of 1928—to outlaw war itself. Neither these legalistic formulas nor the moralistic sentiments sufficed to spare the world from a second global conflict. They did contribute to a false sense of security, however. As a consequence, Americans awoke to an ominous world in the late thirties.

In today's post–Cold War era, America is again pushing free trade and economic integration as a means to worldwide harmony. Globalization is this age's shibboleth. Although prosperity and interdependence are important dimensions of international cooperation, they alone cannot ensure peaceful relations among states. Trade does not occur in a vacuum.

An internationalist posture is all the more imperative as the United States grapples with the evolving multipolar world. The geopolitical vacuum in the immediate post–Cold War years is now giving way to a resurgence of great power politics amid extreme nationalistic and religious fervor. Evidence of this reconfiguration is seen in the policies of a neoimperializing Russia, an ascending China, an emerging India, a widening restiveness within the European Union, and a rising militant form of Islam. Each of these political entities is reaching out to states in their respective geographical spheres and beyond. During the 1990s, the United States had the luxury of choosing between international engagement or disengagement without worrying about major player consequences. The chessboard now has more determined pieces in the game. The new circumstances also permit secondary power—Japan, Germany, and Iran—more latitude than within Cold War constraints. Pawns as well as queens can now influence the game.

Missed and Seized Opportunities in the Post-Cold War Era

No period in its history has offered the Untied States more opportunities for shaping international politics for American ends than the years immediately following the fall of the Berlin Wall. Even after World War II, the United States enjoyed much less freedom, for its postwar plans soon bumped up against the Soviet Union's Central European dominance and, later, its global ambitions. But over the past decade Washington has considered economic globalization and political self-determination as ends themselves rather than as means to larger ends.

On the face of it, the United States has been hyperaggressively exercising power abroad since the Soviet Union's breakdown. Washington kicked off the decade with the deployment of more than a half million ground troops in the Persian Gulf, and ended it by unleashing significant air power in the Kosovo campaign. It fired missiles at Sudan and Afghanistan in retaliation for terrorist attacks. It ousted the Haitian military junta and steamed war ships into Taiwanese waters to put the Chinese on notice for launching rockets during the island's first direct presidential election.

But none of these operations succeeded in disarming a superweapons threat—Iraq and North Korea persist in their dangerous course of furtively developing weapons of mass destruction. Nor have any peacekeeping missions secured a durable political order without an ongoing U.S. military presence. When the United States has made use of its awesome military prowess, it has been applied so tentatively that it has hobbled its impact—just look at predemocratic Serbia, post–Gulf War Iraq, or the nest of terrorist networks in the Middle East. As a result, there have been spectacular displays of techno-warfare without decisive political victories.

A vacillating diplomacy is unlikely to impress determined rulers in China or Russia as it failed to in Milosevic's Serbia, Iraq, or various terrorist cells. This brand of internationalism should be discredited as ineffective and cosmetic posturing. America serves as *the* key guarantor of an open global framework. Washington must work within the international system to ensure a fellowship of free nations and to prevent a major conflict. But in the final analysis, the United States must look to its own devices, not trusting in foreign princes or fanciful diplomacy. Its leadership, nevertheless, can be translated thorough collective bodies and coalition approaches, as has been the case with NATO.

Regional Concerns

South Asia and the Asia-Pacific Regions

Two global regions in particular could have benefited from sustained U.S. attention in the early post–Cold War decade—South Asia and Asia-Pacific. In southern Asia, terrorism in Afghanistan and Pakistan now grabs attention. But little diplomatic enterprise has been devoted to these states despite their importance for oil and natural gas reserves in the Middle East and Central Asia. After the Reagan administration made Afghanistan a front-line state to turn back Soviet expansion, and then Bush repulsed Iraq's invasion of Kuwait, Washington let the larger region languish. When the Afghan *mujahideen* ousted the Soviet puppet regime in Kabul in 1992, conditions were ripe for outside diplomatic intervention to forge a coalition of neighboring states.

It has been U.S. policy since Truman to help a war-torn state recover, particularly one that played a pivotal role in the defeat of an adversary. But the United States failed to act to suspend arms flow into Afghanistan, or to integrate it and surrounding states into a mutual cooperation and development plan. And thus, Afghan society festered. This violent arena is now a breeding ground for terrorism and instability throughout the region and beyond.

The Asia-Pacific region also stood open for a comprehensive diplomatic architecture after the folding of Soviet power. Unlike Europe, where there is a veritable alphabet soup of supranational organizations and abundant interstate consultation, the Pacific rim lacks comparable region-wide organizations. The linkages are unilateral rather than multilateral, and they usually run through Washington.

The Asia Pacific Economic Cooperation forum offered a rudimentary structure that ought to have been strengthened and expanded to bridge the diplomatic gaps. Organized in 1989, APEC began as an informal dialogue group to promote open trade and practical economic cooperation. Now, with twenty-one members and more than 40 percent of global trade, APEC represents a wide and fast-developing array of countries dedicated to transpacific business and trade. At his first APEC meeting, Clinton hinted at a political role for APEC to "foster regional harmony" so as to develop a "community of shared interest."[1]

1. President William J. Clinton, speech at the first APEC Leaders Meeting, Blake Island, Washington, 20 November 1993.

But nothing happened. Without firm American leadership, APEC passed up an opportunity to transform its member countries' economic relations. Even with modest beginnings, much like the European Coal and Steel Community, it could broaden its agenda beyond free trade to financial issues like a common currency and an Asian version of the International Monetary Fund.

In the realm of security, the Association of Southeast Asian Nations (ASEAN) Regional Forum (ARF), which began its annual dialogue in 1994, could serve as an Asian nucleus—if not a Pacific NATO then an Organization for Security and Cooperation in Europe.[2] Whereas NATO had the "glue" of a common Soviet threat to weld it together at its creation, the OSCE includes Russia and strives to bridge the Cold War divide by promoting confidence and security building, human rights, and preventive diplomacy.

After the collapse of Soviet-American bipolarity, the international environment was open for a vibrant Pacific-wide structure devoted to economic, diplomatic, and security issues. The geopolitical window is closing on these once-promising concepts to facilitate contacts and mutual understanding. Instead, the bitter bilateral antagonisms that have plagued China, Japan, and other states for the past hundred years are resurfacing. Had a page been lifted from post–WWII European history, the Pacific would be better prepared organizationally to address resurgent rivalries.

A new Washington government might still address a transpacific framework, which offers a mechanism for the United States to exert leadership without relying solely on unilateral actions. One aim is to enmesh China within the international community as the West incorporated Germany after World War II. Another objective is not to per-

2. ARF covers ASEAN members Brunei, Cambodia, Indonesia, Laos, Malaysia, Myanmar, the Philippines, Singapore, Thailand, and Vietnam and their dialogue partners, Australia, Canada, China, the European Union, India, Japan, Mongolia, New Zealand, North Papua New Guinea, Russia, South Korea, and the United States.

mit China to fashion frameworks that exclude Washington, as is now underway with ASEAN-Plus 3, which includes China, Japan, and South Korea, but not the United States.

Somalia and Beyond

Somalia witnessed the first major post–Cold War intervention exclusively for humanitarian reasons. Begun by Bush a little more than a year after the Persian Gulf war, the Somali operation was initiated to provide food to starving people. The United Nations assumed command in May 1993. But President Clinton reintervened and set forth broader goals of "nation building," conducted with the help of the UN, in the name of "assertive multilateralism." The operation turned sour with this "mission creep." The White House dispatched U.S. troops to capture Mohammed Farrah Aidid, a recalcitrant warlord, who disrupted food distribution and ambushed Pakistani UN troops. Soon, Somalia became a foreign policy debacle, when U.S. soldiers veered from handing out food to street fighting.

Concerned about his popularity and domestic agenda, Clinton decided to pull all U.S. troops out of the northeast African country. In retrospect, it would have been wiser to sidestep such protracted goals as political reconciliation and democratic governance in a clan-torn country so remote to American interests. It was doubly unwise to use underequipped U.S. troops as a police force against neighborhood criminals. But once casualties were taken, it would have been far better to deal appropriately with Aidid, and then turn Somalia back over to the United Nations. The precipitous U.S. withdrawal signaled irresolution and encouraged lawlessness as cold-blooded rulers around the world took note. Unrestrained strongmen, left unchecked, massacred thousands in Central Africa, Southeastern Europe, and the Sudan.

Elsewhere in Africa, the United States not only failed to respond to the 1994 Rwandan massacres but also blocked the UN Security Council from taking action. American-supplied airlift and logistical support could have lessened the carnage that ultimately claimed some eight-hundred thousand Tutsi lives at the hands of roving Hutu militias. Small numbers of UN troops could have halted the Hutus from hacking their victims to death. Just as the United States later furnished Australian peacekeepers transport and intelligence assets in the Indonesian island of East Timor in 1999, Washington could have lent resources while keeping U.S. troops directly out of the fray.

Like Afghanistan and the Asia-Pacific, here was another area ripe for indirect U.S. intervention, which could have also helped stabilize conflicts that erupted in Central and West Africa soon after the Rwandan massacre. The Clinton administration tentatively launched another supranational coalition—an embryonic regional force—what became known as the African Crisis Response Initiative. ACRI brought together African countries with the goal of forming a continental peacekeeping unit. The Pentagon provided limited equipment and training for peacekeeping battalions, command of which remained in the hands of the five respective governments.

The ACRI has labored under the burdens of inadequate resources, slow start-up, and restrictive missions that barred it from fighting local combatants to enforce peace. The concept remains sound. It makes more sense to have African troops intervene in the continent's civil wars than U.S. soldiers. Implementation, however, has been less than wholehearted. Washington also separately furnished funds and assistance to Nigeria for its peacekeeping campaign in conflict-torn Sierra Leone. Again, such indirect efforts lend American assistance and expertise without deploying U.S. ground forces into the pathologies of every ethnic battleground.

Rogue States

Iraq

Rogue states (now termed "states of concern" by the U.S. State Department) dramatically came to center stage in early post–Cold War years with threats chiefly from Iraq and North Korea.[3] Rogue regimes are generally defined as states that refuse to abide by traditional international norms, preferring instead to threaten neighbors with attacks, engage in or sponsor terrorism, promote radical ideologies, develop weapons of mass destruction, and suppress their citizens' human and civil rights.

Iraq captured world attention after a U.S.-led coalition handily pushed Iraqi invaders out of Kuwait in early 1991. Reluctant to advance onto Iraqi soil because it feared another Vietnam or territorial fragmentation of the fragile Iraqi state, the Bush administration left Saddam Hussein in power to pursue evil. Bush called for an army coup or a popular uprising against the corrupt but weakened dictator. When the southern Shiite-dominated region did revolt, Washington left the rebels to the tender mercies of Baghdad rather than aiding insurrection. Neither Bush nor Clinton forcefully backed internal opposition to Hussein—the only realistic option for a regime change.

After Saddam Hussein's defeat in Kuwait, Kurds and Shiites in the north formed the Iraqi National Congress, which set up a semiautonomous community. Lying within the UN no-fly zone, the INC was also protected by lightly armed American infantry under Operation Provide Comfort. The INC disseminated anti-Saddam propaganda, collected intelligence, and established a fledgling political apparatus that received limited CIA support. It represented the one promising effort to undermine Baghdad's hold on the region.

In hopes of resolving differences with the Iraqi dictator, however, the incoming Clinton presidency first reduced funding for the INC and then deserted it. Kurdish factionalism enabled Saddam to divide and conquer what had become known as Kurdistan. Despite being a UN "safe haven" and having prior U.S. backing, Washington largely stood aside when Iraqi tanks rolled into the Kurdish enclave. Hussein's

3. For more on rogue states, see Thomas H. Henriksen, *Using Power and Diplomacy to Deal with Rogue States* (Hoover Institution Press, 1999).

agents extirpated the INC networks, destroyed the resistance base, and murdered scores of INC adherents. Baghdad repaid American passivity by stepping up its quest for weapons of mass destruction and missiles. Neither UN arms inspectors nor almost daily American and British bombing stopped Hussein from pursuing his goal.

Only an internal coup or revolt has any prospect of bringing down Hussein. Clinton signed a 1998 bill designating $97 million to build an opposition but has spent only $20,000 of these funds as of this writing—and for training in civil-military relations, at that. For his tepid actions, Clinton has faced growing criticism at the end of his presidency, especially in light of unrest in the Middle East. A new administration ought to encourage opposition to Hussein by returning to the earlier plan of backing Iraqi dissidents.

Yugoslavia and the Return of the Balkan Turmoil

Soon after the Gulf conflict, horrific civil strife erupted in Yugoslavia, which had been cobbled together from arch-nationalistic ministates that engulfed the Balkans in bloodshed and chaos for decades prior to WWI. As Communist rule receded, ethnic republics reclaimed the independence they possessed at the breakup of the Austro-Hungarian empire. While Slovenia and Macedonia escaped Belgrade's clutches, other ethnonationalities encountered bloody Serbian reprisals starting in 1991. Fighting in Croatia and Bosnia-Herzegovina soon approached World War II brutality. Abetted by Serbian president Slobodan Milo-sevic, local Serb communities attacked Bosnian Muslims and Croats and "ethnically cleansed" them from their homes so as to create a Greater Serbia. Despite criticism from members of his own party, the Bush White House sat on its hands as the casualties mounted in Sarajevo and other Bosnian Muslim enclaves.

President-elect Clinton signaled a tough line toward Serb atrocities but then failed to act for nearly three years. The delay cost some two hundred thousand lives and damaged NATO's credibility. Despite the fact that southeastern Europe adjoins the NATO border and severe political turmoil nearby endangered the alliance and the continent itself, the Clinton White House, in a reprise of the Somali smoke-screen, chose to blame the United Nations for ineffectiveness. Not until the beginning of the 1996 reelection campaign when Republican presidential challenger Bob Dole made Yugoslavia a political issue, did Clinton initiate a counterresponse. Finally, America took the lead in a NATO bombing campaign, which buttressed Croatia's ground offensive and stopped Serb assaults.

To its credit, Washington indirectly undertook training Croatian forces to rebuff a Serb onslaught by hiring a private company that schooled officers in military strategy. Military Professional Resources, Inc. was founded in 1987 by former high-ranking U.S. generals. Based in Alexandria, Virginia, MPRI received a State Department contract to train Croatian officers. Armed with weapons purchased from the international market as well as smuggled Iranian stocks, Croatian troops rolled back the Serbs. By allowing those with a cause at stake to fight their own battles, the United States adopted the correct prescription.

Reeling from the Croatian counteroffensive, the Bosnian Serbs agreed to an America-brokered settlement, the Dayton Accord. But this accord drew its inspiration from the politics of multiculturalism, a difficult sell in a country lacking a democratic tradition or lasting heritage of tolerance. As a result, the United States and its European allies now must garrison Bosnia for the indefinite future.

In retrospect, sounder politics called for more or less ethnic homogeneity within separate states rather than artificial constructs of multiethnicity. Such entities would have been more in sync with the historical realities and global trends, and more durable than the fragile and volatile Muslim-Croat federation of Bosnia-Herzegovina, which encompasses the Republika Srpska, a Serb ministate.

Not long after Dayton, trouble erupted in Kosovo, a Serbian province. Again, a region bordering Central Europe was being subjected to state-run terror against Muslims, a minority in southeastern Europe but a majority in Kosovo. Once the Rambouillet talks broke down between Serbs and Muslims, Belgrade stepped up its killing and expelling of Kosovar Albanians.

Under American leadership, NATO counterpunched with a bombing assault in late March 1999 that lasted seventy-eight days. Although the air campaign eventually severed Serb control of Kosovo, the conduct of the conflict lacked textbook precision. Due to the faintheartedness of some European states (mostly France, Italy, and Greece), Washington throttled back on the air onslaught. As a result, NATO incrementally applied its air power and failed to halt the expulsion of ethnic Albanians or convince Milosevic to quickly surrender.

Washington misjudged Belgrade, believing it would buckle as rapidly as it did under NATO's pinprick air attacks in the summer of 1995. But that bombing in reality supported a fierce Croatian land assault on Serb strongholds. No such land assault accompanied the Kosovo bombing campaign. NATO should have deployed ground troops in Albania, Hungary, and Macedonia to underscore its resolve before the air war began. It also chose not to arm the Kosovo Liberation Army, a fledgling resistance movement. This time-honored practice of having local forces fight their own cause was spurned amid rumors that the KLA harbored criminal elements.

This humanitarian war bred a string of ironies. To begin with, the air strikes actually accentuated reprisals against the ethnic Albanians. Nearly a million fled to neighboring states before drifting back after Milosevic accepted the Balkans military agreement. Then, as Belgrade withdrew its troops from Kosovo, it was the Serbs' turn to flee. Fearing—correctly—Muslim retaliation, two-thirds of them left. Kosovo became a virtual NATO protectorate, free of former Serbian rule.

Unless NATO plans an indefinite colonial presence in Kosovo, the only practical solution is to prepare it for sovereignty within its present borders. The Kosovars will not accept anything less than their own independent state, and the *status quo* invites persistent civil strife. Failing implementation of such a blueprint, the United States should gradually withdraw its forces from Kosovo and Bosnia and turn over peacekeeping duties to the European Union and states like Canada and Sweden.

The overriding Balkans lesson is the fallacy of negotiating with ruthless tyrants. Ample instruction was at hand from dealings with Saddam Hussein, if not previous dictators. After the Dayton agreement, Milosevic was soon stirring up ethnic trouble in Kosovo, curtailing political rights within Serbia, and fomenting problems in Montenegro, the last remaining republic within the Serb state in the former Yugoslavia. Had the United States backed anti-Milosevic demonstrations during the 1996–97 winter, it might have sooner precipitated the rise to power of democratic forces in Serbia. Just as the Solidarity trade union, when aided by President Reagan, undermined communist rule in Poland, so too the budding democratic movement in Serbia ousted Milosevic dictatorship.[4]

North Korea

Across the globe in East Asia, the United States confronted another unfriendly regime, which also survived and even profited from Washington's tepid response. North Korea, the insular Stalinesque relic of the Cold War, heightened tension with its nuclear plans. Since the Korean War, a state of war had existed between North and South. Along the demilitarized zone (DMZ) separating the two states, each government stationed powerful armed forces on hair-trigger alert. When Clinton took office, it was becoming clear to Washington that Pyongyang had embarked on nuclear weapons development in violation of the Nonproliferation Treaty, which it signed in 1985.

By late 1993, it was widely assumed that the North had already manufactured atomic bombs, or at minimum had the capability to do so in the near future. Rather than sticking to a deterrence formula to address Pyongyang's nuclear threat, the Clinton administration bro-

4. For more on the use of outside support to promote democracy, see Thomas H. Henriksen, "Covert Operations, Now More Than Ever," *Orbis* (winter 2000): 145–56.

kered the Agreed Framework, an arms control agreement signed in Geneva in October 1994. Under this agreement, Pyongyang promised to suspend its atomic weapons program, leave its plutonium rods in place, and permit international inspection of some nuclear reactor facilities. The United States, in turn, persuaded South Korea and Japan to fund construction of two light water reactors to replace the North's Soviet-designed graphite reactors. Until the new nuclear plants came online, Clinton pledged to supply annually half a million metric tons of fuel oil to generate electrical power north of the DMZ.

In mid-1998, North Korea upped the blackmail ante by launching a three-stage rocket that traversed Japanese territory before plunging thousands of miles away into the Pacific. Anxiously, Seoul and Washington stepped up engagement initiatives and aid packages rather than relying on deterrence. North Korea, battered by floods, droughts, and scant exports, looked to Western largesse to replace Moscovite assistance that ended with the Soviet collapse. Its calculated gamble succeeded.

The Clinton administration's prescription ran into withering criticism. Detractors charged that the Agreed Framework was unverifiable because North Korea limited inspectors' access to nuclear facilities. Outsiders, therefore, could not guarantee that Pyongyang had really suspended the development of nuclear weapons. Even defenders of Clinton had to admit the deal established a dangerous precedent by giving into nuclear blackmail with a rogue state.

Later, when the issue of building an antimissile system surfaced in U.S. domestic politics in early 2000, the Agreed Framework helped undercut the argument that deterrence could be substituted for National Missile Defense. Skeptics of NMD argued that instead of a missile defense the United States had the option of deterring a nuclear missile attack by threatening massive retaliation. But in a ready-made dress rehearsal for this scenario, Washington blinked by negotiating the agreement, thereby vitiating the deterrence argument.

Proponents for the Geneva accord, however, claimed it secured a peaceful resolution of nuclear standoff in 1994. Less than five years later, Pyongyang mounted a diplomatic offense, opening relations first with Italy and then a string of nations. Unexpectedly, it agreed to a head-of-state summit with South Korean president Kim Dae Jung, who had unveiled a "sunshine," or engagement, policy toward the North. Kim Jong-il, the North Korean leader, outwardly appeared at the June 2000 summit in Pyongyang as a jovial man with whom the world could do business.

The possibility of a genuine thaw on the Korean peninsula would have far-reaching consequences for the United States and China as well as surrounding states. Questions would surface in Washington and Beijing about the need for 37,000 U.S. troops in South Korea, if military tensions ease. A total or partial withdrawal of the American presence, in turn, would spell strategic changes. Ironically, will a reduction of tension on the peninsula also sharpen the view of China as the main security threat in East Asia? With North Korea no longer serving as the bête noire, China's arms buildup will receive more scrutiny.

While rogue nations (or "states of concern") captured much media and policy attention in the 1990s, they were gradually overshadowed by larger political realities in China, Russia, and the European Union as these entities pushed their own agendas. These changes could not be more portentous for the international strategic balance.

Great Power Politics

Russia: A Recovering Great Power

Unlike the German and Japanese defeat in 1945, the Soviet Union's disintegration was less traumatic. Soviet cities still stood. No occupation army garrisoned the country. But a seventy-year regime dissolved into political and ideological bankruptcy. Large swaths of territory and millions of non-Russians split off from the defunct Soviet Union and formed independent nations in the Baltics, Central Asia, and the southern Caucasus. Despite the losses, or perhaps because of them, Russians yearned for democracy and free markets as a salvation to their plight.

Eager to convert Russia into the ranks of new democracies and even embrace it as a "strategic partner," the Clinton administration turned a blind eye to corruption, rewarded its power holders, and bailed out incompetence with approval of billions of dollars in loans from the International Monetary Fund, the World Bank, U.S. Export-Import Bank and other American governmental entities. Much of this largesse became ill-gotten gains and were transferred to accounts in Switzerland and Cyprus.

Washington could have mixed carrots and sticks to prod and prompt Moscow toward a genuine pluralistic system with democratic institutions. Humanitarian aid administered to the Russian people directly, as Herbert Hoover independently managed food relief in the 1920s, would have been more effective. Direct contacts and exchanges from the U.S. Congress to the Russian Duma would have also done more to further democracy in the early 1990s than strictly state-to-state relations. Reminiscent of postwar training of young Germans and Japanese officials, the Library of Congress in 1999 embarked on the instruction of 2000 Russian officials that is worthy of broadening.

The Kremlin's bureaucratic thievery eviscerated the Russian economy as well as slowed its reform. Former Communist bosses grabbed hold of industries, turning themselves into superrich oligarchs in the new Russia. By tying itself to the failing Boris Yeltsin, whose mixture of anarchic and authoritarian rule gave Washington wide latitude, the United States contributed to the discrediting of democracy, free markets, and Western-influenced reformers among many Russians.

At the start of the new millennium, Russia has come to rest in a quasi-democratic limbo, somewhere closer to authoritarian rule than Western-style democracy. Washington certainly made its wishes widely known to China by criticizing Beijing democratic and human rights lapses. But with Russia, it often rewarded the Yeltsin presidency without demanding reforms or conditioning assistance on good governance.

Clinton praised Vladimir Putin's election in March 2000 as the first Russian democratic transfer in nearly a thousand years. The truth is that when Yeltsin resigned the presidency to Putin, the former president, in effect, engineered a political campaign against which no other candidate stood a chance. Later in the year, evidence came to light of massive voter fraud. Thus, Putin's election itself was far from a genuine democratic transition. By manipulating a second bloody war in the breakaway Chechen republic to his political advantage, Putin demonstrated a ruthlessness that belied hope for a benign post-Soviet Russia. His crackdown on media freedom and pursuit of centralizing governance raised caution flags about the future of a democratic and peaceful Russia.

With Putin, Russia has an autocratic leader. And the United States faces a reassertive Russia, albeit one weakened by a still-poor economy and embattled by Muslim separatist revolts. But together with China, which Moscow courts, Russia seeks to be a major power in the new international order, reasserting influence, if not rule, in former Soviet territories. Russo-American friction will be played out in the Baltics, Central Asia, and the Caucasus. Washington can expand nongovernmental initiatives and educate a younger generation in the rule of law and democracy. It is in America's interest that the new countries in these regions preserve their sovereignty. But it is up to each to develop their economies and enhance their own state-building progress.

As the world moves from East-West bipolarism, European restiveness with Washington's tutelage is altering political contours. Europe's policies toward Moscow will shape the future, largely independent of Washington's orientation. Despite Russia's protest over the 1999 NATO enlargement to include Poland, Hungary, and the Czech Republic—which is proving to be a prudent decision—Russia must look to Europe for assistance. At a minimum, Russia needs European funds to rebuild its industries.

Russian designs are much larger, however. Putin has already un-veiled a diplomatic offensive to split Germany, the linchpin of the continent, from the Atlantic alliance. He sought to interest the Ger-man Chancellor, Gerhard Schroeder, in a Russo-European antimissile system. The Russian president's visit to European capitals in June 2000 succeeded in exacerbating tensions between Europe and Washington over missile defense, which Europeans opposed. Muscovy policy is aimed at tilting Europe away from Washington. Moscow meddling might also widen the emerging Franco-German split. A new American administration will need to counter Russian maneuvers in order to preserve the pro-American focus of the Atlantic alliance.

In the next millennium, the United States needs to reevaluate the criteria under which it gives economic aid to Russia. Conditioning assistance on the existence of core democratic institutions such as a free press and independent corruption watchdogs, as Larry Diamond in this volume has suggested, is one option. Filtering money through nongovernmental organizations, which train and educate citizens to carry on reforms themselves is another—one which does greater long-term good then simply doling out block grants. In addition, the United States needs to "get personal" with the oil oligarchs now controlling the country. The oligarchs, who threaten not only Russia's transition to democracy but also the international rule of law through their crim-inal activity, should be treated like pariahs and denied international capital.[5] The business-as-usual approach with Russia deserves to be discarded because it contributed to a kleptocracy that undermines the foundations for liberal democracy.

China: The Looming Competitor

With the world's largest population and the grand sweep of its five-thousand-year civilization, China's geopolitical weight has long been

---

5. For more on this viewpoint, see Lee S. Wolosky, "Putin's Plutocrat Problem," *Foreign Affairs* 79, No. 2 (March/April 2000): 18–31.

recognized in foreign capitals. China's status swelled during the past decade, as its economic growth stood in marked contrast to Russia's steep decline. Rather than containing or constricting Chinese development, the United States since the Nixon administration gradually sought to engage China. A prosperous, politically plural, and militarily secure China, recent administrations argued, would be a peaceful and constructive member of the international community. The logic ran that if China were commercially embraced then liberal democracy would follow.

But prospects of amicable relations with China were undercut by ambiguous implementation of the engagement policy. Good trade relations seemed at first to infuse Washington's policy. But the Clinton administration hesitated and its inconsistencies created doubt in Beijing.

On the most crucial economic issue between the two countries, China's permanent normal trade relations (PNTR) with the United States, which would further Beijing's admittance into the World Trade Organization, Clinton vacillated. In April 1999, when a deal was tantalizingly near, he rejected an attractive Chinese offer because of domestic pressure from his own party and labor unions. The mistaken NATO bombing of Beijing's embassy in Belgrade during the Kosovo conflict inflamed Chinese hostility toward Americans. The twin errors roiled Sino-American relations. Seven months after the U.S. rejection, the president managed to resurrect the PNTR negotiations but on a slightly less-favorable basis.

This time around, Clinton overrode his party and relied on Republican votes in the House. There was really no other choice but to welcome China's economic arrival into the comity of nations and to smooth its transition to a more open and peaceful society. Excluding it from the global economy would have created decades of resentment and opposition to the United States. After passage of PNTR, Beijing-Washington relations fundamentally altered, for China was no longer subject to annual Congressional reviews of its human rights, labor practices, and environmental lapses.

Detractors of normalization predicted that open trade would contribute to building an expansionist China with a powerful military force. China would become such a powerful regional player that no major international action could be taken without first considering Beijing reaction. Already, this is the case in East Asia, where Vietnam, to cite one example, awaits China's entry into the WTO before advancing it own case. In short, China will revert to its historic position in which tributary or weak states surround the Middle Kingdom.

Proponents of greater economic intercourse with China held that development would broaden the middle class, and strengthen democratic elements, thereby enhancing peaceful relations. They cite the democratic transition of such states as Chile, Spain, South Korea, and Taiwan that followed in the wake of material improvement. Time will settle the debate.

But in the meantime, China perceives itself as encircled by an American alliance system. Opposed to the United States' guarantees to Taiwan, and recent defense guidelines with Japan, China has launched an arms buildup. With Beijing's increasing missile batteries opposite Taiwan, and naval inroads in the South China Seas, U.S. defense planners will have to keep a close eye on Chinese behavior.

China's ascendancy is being accompanied by Beijing's ambitions to dominate East Asia. The return of Hong Kong and Macao to Chinese rule represents the first steps. Control over Taiwan is another. Judging by history, China's strategy will extend to everything from clandestine operations to military assault to reestablish a Sino-centered shadow over its neighbors.

China's behind-the-scenes engineering of North Korea into a somewhat less-menacing state is best understood as a strategy to erode justification for U.S. forces in South Korea or for a U.S. antimissile system in the region. Once the troops have withdrawn, the Korea peninsula will revert to its historical role of being subordinate to Chinese influence. This in turn places Japan in precarious straits, particularly if Tokyo remains relatively disarmed and ambivalent about U.S. military presence.

Beijing's naval projection into the South China Sea and control over some of the Spratly Islands portend ongoing friction with its Asian neighbors and the United States. The newborn Sino-Russian cordiality enables Beijing to focus its attention southward toward the sea instead of its northern border. It has gained a strategic foothold in Myanmar on the Indian Ocean. China's maritime aspirations, however, have provoked the apprehension of India, which among other defensive steps has agreed to assist in rebuilding Vietnam's navy.

The rise of China beyond its contemporary status as a capable regional power will present Washington with its greatest foreign policy challenge in the coming decades. China will be neither a partner nor an adversary during the first decade of the twenty-first century. As candidate George W. Bush avowed during the 2000 presidential campaign, China will be a " strategic competitor." It is almost a foregone conclusion that China will economically and politically dominate the region similar to American sway over the Caribbean—small states will defer to it. China should be judged on its political and military behavior. Military adventures or direct subjugation of neighbors would demand a more robust policy than the engagement course sketched in this chapter.

Washington's posture must be to reassure Japan and South Korea that the American presence in East Asia is there for the long haul. Japan, America's best ally in the region, should be encouraged to play a greater role in East Asia. How China evolves will determine the balance of American policy. At this point, the optimum approach for the United States is a judicious mix of economic engagement and political accommodation, but military deterrence from aggression.

Europe: A Global Player Again?

Until World War II devastated Europe, the continent had been the international system's center of gravity for over three hundred years. Atlantic Europe, indeed, conquered much of the globe, spreading colonial rule, trade networks, commercial enterprises, and cultural and linguistic zones across much of the planet. Europe's second civil war in the twentieth century destroyed this epicenter. As a consequence, Europe lost overseas lands, surrendered imperial aspirations, and saw its influence eclipsed by U.S. and Soviet power.

Once the Soviet threat of invasion ceased, European reliance on American arms, it was predicted, would soon subside. Yet the Balkan wars revealed that without Washington, the Europeans could not handle a crisis in their own backyard. Among the ironies of the U.S. intervention, in fact, was that it provoked West European resentment. Worse yet, Euro-nationalism is currently defined by an opposition to the United States, which is viewed as a "hyperpower" by the envious French. French hostility toward the United States has played out in frequent vetoes against American initiatives in the UN Security Council—for example, the French voted against tougher U.S. actions against Iraq.

The Kosovo campaign gave greater salience to twin issues—burden sharing and power sharing—confronting the transatlantic alliance since its inception. NATO and the European Union have chafed at Washington's commanding dominance of the Atlantic alliance. The United States, for its part, has long pressed Europe to spend more and spend smarter on defense. In short, even though it faces no exterior threat, the American-European partnership is under strain.

Kosovo served as a catalyst to the EU summit meeting at Helsinki in December 1999. The EU member states pledged to field a force of sixty thousand trained rapid-reaction troops by 2003 that can be mobilized within sixty days. Kosovo also prompted European governments to invest in state-of-the-art weaponry. Doubts, however, linger on both sides of the Atlantic as to whether Helsinki goals will be realized. In the short term, this burgeoning EU assertiveness stems from deepening economic confidence in the fifteen-nation bloc and from growing aspirations to play a greater role in world affairs beyond U.S. dominance. But so far its effectiveness has not matched its appetite.

Unless the continent pulls its own weight, U.S. disenchantment will be fed by the disparity between American and European military power. As Washington's attention is drawn toward China and the transpacific arena, the United States will be compelled to nudge Europe toward greater self-reliance. At the same time, the Eurocrats are in an antihegemonist posture, criticizing the United States for its global ascendancy. This will require Washington to both encourage European military self-sufficiency while not inflaming anti-Americanism. This is not a new story in NATO, although the rise of the European Union gives it greater potency. In short, the Cold War goal remains the same: a prosperous and free Europe that is a strong partner in the Atlantic alliance.

The Road Ahead

The post–Cold War era—characterized by the lessening of major power politics—is ending. We have begun to move to another, as yet unnamed, period. The early post-Soviet years witnessed a strategic imbalance resulting from the sudden implosion of Moscow's vast empire. This disequilibrium no longer pertains.

Neither Russia nor China views itself as solely a regional power. Both seek to compete globally with the United States. Both export arms and advanced technology to worrisome states like Iran, Iraq, North Korea, and Pakistan. They sidled up to each other so as to give reality to a renascent Sino-Russian entente that suggests a great-power triangle. India asserts itself diplomatically and militarily in adjoining areas. The EU hungers for a greater international role on the international stage. The post-Wall strategic vacuum is filling with political crosscurrents and new ambitions.

India is also fast assuming a larger geopolitical role. The economic, demographic, and democratic significance of India has only begun to be noted in Washington. India's location in South Asia, proximity to China, growing economy, and respected military capacity make it an appealing U.S. partner. In the next decade, the United States must establish a closer relationship with New Delhi. India's troubled relations with China should also give it standing with a United States concerned about China's ambitions.

Weapons of mass destruction and ballistic missiles during the East-West standoff were confined largely to a small number of major powers, which looked to international agreements to maintain a nuclear balance. Today, the proliferation of rockets and nuclear components to unfriendly regimes poses a grave threat to the United States and many other countries and demands a reconsideration of policy options. Atomic weapons capacity is becoming a global reality. India and Pakistan, neither of which are rogue states, joined the membership of declared nuclear states by testing devices in 1998. The United States must recalibrate its policies to take account of these changing realities. Arms control treaties, created for the symmetrical Cold War power relationship, are no longer as effective against big-power supplied rogues, who ignore legal niceties. This emerging threat makes some sort of missile shield a categorical imperative.

Washington must redouble its diplomatic exertions to halt the patronage of rogue dictators, when dealing with Russia and China. It is not enough just to engage Moscow and Beijing commercially with the aim of guiding them toward free markets, democracy, and peaceful relations among big powers. Stopping the export of missile and nuclear technology must be part of the negotiation process. It must also pursue forceful diplomacy that divides patrons from rogue regimes, thus neutralizing such regimes.

Because circumstances differ with each rogue, the steps to be taken against them can vary from muscular covert actions that topple dictators to economic and diplomatic engagement. One minimalist but long-term approach entails diplomatic and material aid to shadow governments either inside or outside the rogue regimes. But whatever the course of action, it must be sustained beyond the poll-driven photo-op approach so characteristic of the Clinton presidency.

With respect to failed states that implode, causing misery and death for their inhabitants, the past is prologue. There will probably be more of these, particularly in Africa. Colombia, Pakistan, Indonesia, and post-Castro Cuba could also join the ranks of catastrophic human tragedies. While the United States cannot make lambs lie down with lions, it has to intervene in some civil disorders, such as the Balkans, because they adjoin regions central to American interests. If the United States always stood aside, its cherished values would be discredited; damage to American prestige and credibility will undercut U.S. interests. Extravagant crusades for democracy or human rights cannot be sustained but neither can a policy of blanket nonintervention. It behooves America, however, not to become bogged down in the aftermath of direct military interventions. Mundane police duties are best left to others.

The United States must distinguish between, on the one side, the muscular internationalism of Harry Truman and Ronald Reagan, and the utopian multilateralism of Woodrow Wilson and Bill Clinton on the other. Practical internationalism is critical to preventing war, expanding trade, and promoting democracy and respect for human rights. This leadership can be translated through collective security arrangements and regional frameworks but it cannot be solely reliant on them in all circumstances.

Sticking up for our values does not harm the pursuit of our vital interests, for our values are not distinct from our interests. The realistic promotion of democracy and human rights serves American interests in ways that realpolitik can never accomplish alone. Obviously, the United States cannot ignore the balance of power or the emergence of a power capable of dominating the Eurasian continent. This overriding objective demanded large-scale U.S. politico-military intervention in European affairs three times in the past century. Worst-case scenarios mounted by China or Russia would foreclose American humanitarian endeavors. Until Beijing or Moscow threatens this traditional strategic imperative, Washington has some latitude to pursue other less-vital interests.

America represents ideals of freedom, individual rights, and nonaggression for territorial aggrandizement. So, when these principles are violated, other states look to the American response. The United States cannot react in every case where its principles are flouted. But failing to act is not costless—doubt is cast on whether the United States will defend its interests as well as its principles.

This does not represent a strategy for hegemony. The charge of American hegemonism is spurious and motivated by power envy. The United States cannot hide its power. Nor should it. The exercise of American power from time to time will not lead inexorably to a law of political physics whereby states always coalesce against the top dog in antihegemonist entente. This is because the United States, unlike Nazi Germany or Soviet Russia, is not bent on endangering others' independence or freedom.

Trade, human interchange, information flows, and international bodies can facilitate peace in many circumstances; these conditions alone, however, do not preserve American interests or guarantee a war-free planet. America's global engagement undergirds the international system.

The global activism advocated in this chapter cannot be undertaken with the current shrunken military forces. Current expenditures for defense, diplomacy, intelligence, and foreign assistance amounts to slightly more than $325 billion—a large sum, but only 3 percent of our Gross Domestic Product. The Defense Department's budget is about 15 percent of the total federal budget, with a great bulk of funds allocated for Social Security, Medicare, and other nondefense domestic programs.

In rebuilding its defenses, the United States ought not to solely prepare for the humanitarian and peacekeeping operations of the past decade. It must instead look to potential rivals. The Western Pacific demands strategic attention. Ships and planes capable of negotiating the vast oceanic distances are a first priority. The sea lanes around Japan and Indonesia and in the Middle East must be kept open.

Preserving America's preeminent standing is not an end in itself. But the longer the United States holds fast to is position, the longer the world will be hospitable to free markets, political pluralism, and the rule of law. Together, these political currents do as much for averting a global war as they do for extending American principles.

Contra Globalization
and U.S. Hegemony

News weeklies attract readers with lurid, exaggerated covers, and European ones arc no exception. A 1967 *Der Spiegel* cover screamed "Wann Brennt Neu York?" (When Will New York Burn?) accompanied by an illustration of an American ghetto in flames. Thirty years later, with the Soviet empire gone and the United States thriving, *Der Spiegel* named Americans "Herren Der Welt" (Lords of the World), who boasted "We're bathing in our glory." The story within described the United States as a giant beast led by a pompous president who had the nerve to receive European leaders in jeans and a cowboy hat. It complained of the takeover of the world by MTV, Microsoft, and McDonald's (fast music, fast computers, and fast food). "The Americans are acting, in the absence of limits placed on them by anybody or anything, as if they own a blank check in their private McWorld. . . . America is now the Schwarzenegger of international politics: showing off muscles, obtrusive, intimidating."[1]

French President Francois Mitterrand went so far as to declare that "we are at war with America" because the Americans "are voracious, they want undivided power over the world," and his foreign minister urged Europe to "resist with nerves of steel" America's *hyperpuissance*.[2]

1. "Baden wir in unserem Ruhm," *Der Spiegel* (1 September 1997): 160–76.
2. Peter Rodman, *Drifting Apart? Trends in U.S.-European Relations* (Washington, D.C.: The Nixon Center, 1999), p. 55.

However, NATO remains intact, and in June 2000 the Europeans even awarded President Clinton their prestigious Charlemagne prize. But let no one doubt that diplomatic courtesies drape a certain resentment, envy, and fear. And if friends of the United States would not mind seeing it taken down a peg, its potential rivals imagine that American political, business, and military leaders conspire daily to ensure that Russia remains a basket case, China is destabilized, and Islamic culture is perverted by a "made in the U.S.A." materialism.

To be sure, much of the ranting about America's hard and soft power amounts to sour grapes, or is meant for domestic consumption. No one can credibly blame the United States for prevailing in the three global wars of the last century, inventing revolutionary technologies, or releasing the energy and wit of a free people to create goods, services, and entertainment that much of the world craves. But many foreigners, and some Americans, are justifiably worried about what the United States government will choose to do, or not do, with its power. They are eager to learn what grand strategy shapes American policy now that the United States has become not the slayer of beasts, but the beast.

This essay examines the United States' attempts—both past and present—to formulate such a strategy, pointing out the pointlessness of strategic debate as well as the foolishness of current stances. It ends with a lesson from the eleventh century, followed by a prescription for seven assets the United States should cultivate, as opposed to a grand strategy.

The Folly of Strategic Debate

In Republican circles, the answer most often heard to the question of what grand strategy now shapes American policy is that the United States has had no strategy at all since the end of the Cold War, given the flip-flops, false starts, contradictions, and incompetence of the Clinton administration with regard to China, Japan, Russia, the Koreas, the Persian Gulf, the Balkans, and humanitarian interventions.

Supporters of the Clinton administration retort that it is composed of visionaries who "see farther into the future" (as Secretary of State Madeleine Albright boasted), and if it appeared that they had no strategy it is because the new world order and its universal values transcend power politics. So it is that the debate among pundits invariably revisits two questions. Has history entered a globalized era in which the old rules no longer apply? Or, if competing nation-states remain the basic units of the international system, what sort of strategy is correct for the unprecedented "sole superpower?" So far, this debate has been fruitless. It may in fact be a fool's errand.

First, strategy is by its nature secretive, deceptive, and counterintuitive. A statesman would no more announce his strategic intentions in advance than a chess player would hand his opponent a list of his opening moves. Let us say, for the sake of argument, that when Clinton and his advisers sat down after hours over a bottle of Merlot they discussed ways to *preserve* Fidel Castro in power (fearing a chaotic transition), *hamstring* the Taiwanese (lest Beijing go ballistic), manipulate Mexico's presidential election, and sow discord in the councils of Europe. If so, they would not have announced their intentions in an executive session of the Foreign Relations Committee, much less on a Sunday morning talk show.

Second, meaningful strategic discourse must be conducted at the operational level because strategy is a form of economy. A German general once complained that Hitler "was interested in the very big issues, and also in the tiniest details. Anything in between did not interest him. What he overlooked was that most decisions fall into this intermediate category."[3] Hitler's personal foible is a systemic shortcoming of open societies that discuss foreign policy either in terms of vague, benign ends or precise tactics, skirting the realm in which the grave choices are made. For instance, the U.S. Commission on National Security lists criteria to determine when the United States should in-

---

3. Alan Bullock, *Hitler and Stalin: Parallel Lives* (New York: Knopf, 1992), p. 578.

tervene militarily.[4] But they are all elastic. How "imperiled" must our allies be before we should act? At what point does proliferation portend "significant" harm? How many deaths constitute "genocide?" Such imponderables cannot be quantified, nor all contingencies anticipated. And yet, in normal times, such unpredictable or unmentionable issues are precisely the ones an administration must address.

A third reason for the sterility of abstract debate is that strategy is partly reactive. Just as we would not show an opponent our list of intended chess moves, we would be foolish to consult it ourselves for the reason that our plans must change in response to the opponent's moves. It is easy to say that the United States has a vital interest in Northeast Asian stability, and therefore should maintain a forward military presence, promote dialogue between the two Koreas, and enlist the support of Japan and China. But what our operational strategy should be in the event of a crisis is dependent on so many fluid and complex variables that premature discussion is of limited value.

A fourth reason is that democracies are ill-equipped to formulate or execute *any* long-term strategy except in time of war or obvious peril. As Tocqueville famously observed, "Foreign politics demand scarcely any of those qualities which are peculiar to a democracy; they require, on the contrary, the perfect use of almost all those in which it is deficient. . . . [A] democracy can only with great difficulty regulate the details of an important undertaking, persevere in a fixed design, and work out its execution in spite of serious obstacles. It cannot combine its measures with secrecy or await their consequences with patience. These are qualities which more especially belong to an individual or an aristocracy; and they are precisely the qualities by which a nation, like an individual, attains a dominant position."[5] Add to that the fact

4. United States Commission on National Security/21st Century, Phase 2 Report, "Seeking a National Strategy" (15 April 2000), p. 13.
5. Alexis de Tocqueville, *Democracy in America*, vol. 1 (New York: Vintage Books, 1945), pp. 243–44.

that U.S. leadership changes every four to eight years, and that even policy within administrations is perturbed by domestic politics, the media, and a public susceptible to emotion-based appeals, and the unlikelihood of America successfully implementing long-term strategy is clear.

But even if one were to stipulate that strategy *can* be meaningfully debated in public and the nation *can* be rallied to support a long-term design, a fifth objection would render the enterprise moot. In 1994, Henry Kissinger wrote in his magisterial book, *Diplomacy*, that in an international system comprising five or six major powers and many other actors, "order will have to emerge much as it did in past centuries from a reconciliation and balancing of competing national interests." That is, the new world order "is still in a period of gestation, and its final form will not be visible until well into the next century."[6] Strategic thought cannot begin until the environment of potential threats, opportunities, and players and their interests can be discerned. In an era of history defined by relative peace, but also unusual flux and uncertainty, it is wasteful and potentially dangerous to commit to a long-term strategy before one can make confident judgments about the evolution of China and Russia, Japan and South Asia, the Gulf states, and a unified Europe. To be sure, Washington can offer olive branches and good offices to all these states in hopes of influencing the shape of the international order, but it cannot take for granted a panoply of outcomes and devise a strategy based on those assumptions—not yet.

A sixth, and final, reason why our quest for a strategy will lead nowhere is that the American people don't want one. In 1997, I asked David Eisenhower what he thought of the idea that Republicans ought to offer voters an aggressive foreign policy vision. He replied:

6. Henry Kissinger, *Diplomacy* (New York: Simon and Schuster, 1994), pp. 805–6.

On balance, demagoguery is overrated in American politics. The bottom line is that Americans are indifferent about foreign policy for an obvious reason — there is no reason presently to be concerned that U.S. foreign policy is being mismanaged. And that is not a "problem," but a fact of life which some neo-conservatives want to change! In sum, Americans are in a posture of watchful waiting, which is where they ought to be. It would be foolhardy to design a political comeback for conservatism based on a manufactured foreign policy agenda. Americans are well-advised to postpone major decisions about preparedness and strategy until new international patterns show their hand. Seven, eight, ten concepts of the world vie for acceptance among experts, and most of them are plausible. So it would be most un-conservative for Americans to stir things up, which could only result in a weakening of America's international position and in penalties for the party and administration held responsible for bringing that about.[7]

Eisenhower is right. We cannot even guess yet whether the era to come will be characterized by unipolarity, multipolarity, globalization, competitive blocs, power politics, enlargement of market democracy, Third Way regulation, a clash of civilizations, "the democratic peace," zones of order and chaos, "money-grubbing nationalism" (in Harvey Sicherman's phrase), or some combination of the above. That suggests the wisdom of watchful waiting, not ambitious campaigns for new orders that may perversely *damage* the future environment by seeming to confirm other states' fears of America's hegemonic ambitions.

The Lesson of History Is *"pas trop de zêle"*

So far, I have argued that Americans cannot plot long-term strategy at present. Now let us expand on Tocqueville's alleged dictum that democracies can *never* pursue consistent strategy. To begin with, Tocqueville's book suffers the same abuse as the Bible in that its pithiest verses are often quoted out of context and made into proof texts for heresies.

7. Private memorandum to the author.

In fact, he began his foreign policy discussion by noting the very *durable* strategy of nonalignment enunciated in Washington's farewell address. Tocqueville later ended his discussion with a paean to aristocracy.

> Almost all the nations that have exercised a powerful influence upon the destinies of the world, by conceiving, following out, and executing vast designs, from the Romans to the English, have been governed by aristocratic institutions. Nor will this be a subject of wonder when we recollect that nothing in the world is so conservative in its views as an aristocracy. The mass of the people may be led astray by ignorance or passion; the mind of a king may be biased and made to vacillate in his designs, and besides, a king is not immortal. But an aristocratic body is too numerous to be led astray by intrigue, and yet not numerous enough to yield readily to the intoxication of unreflecting passion. An aristocracy is a firm and enlightened body that never dies.[8]

In other words, Tocqueville perceived how the passions and inconstancy of American democracy might cause its foreign policy to lurch spasmodically from passivity to zealous activity and back to passivity. But insofar as a home-grown "aristocracy" represented by the Virginia dynasty enjoyed deference, then an underlying strategic vision might prevail. It was the rise of populism in the Jacksonian era that made Tocqueville skeptical of a democracy's ability to execute strategy. His real lesson was that America can indeed act strategically, but only when an obvious threat exists and the masses are prepared to be led.

What strategic postures has the United States adopted in the past, and what lessons, if any, can be drawn from them? Elsewhere, I have described what I consider the eight enduring traditions of U.S. foreign policy.[9] But in terms of grand strategy they reduce to three. The first great era of American strategic thought lasted from 1776 to 1824, and

8. Tocqueville, *Democracy in America*, p. 245.
9. Walter A. McDougall, *Promised Land, Crusader State: The American Encounter with the World since 1776* (Boston: Houghton Mifflin, 1997). For the "short course" see McDougall, "Back to Bedrock," *Foreign Affairs* (March/April 1997): 134–46.

produced the principles enshrined in the Declaration of Independence and Constitution, Washington's farewell, Jefferson's Second Inaugural, John Quincy Adams's 4 July 1821 speech ("America does not go forth in search of monsters to destroy"), and the Monroe Doctrine. The strategic vision thus defined was of a nation destined to span the continent and penetrate the Pacific—so long as it remained united at home, resisted the temptation to crusade abroad, and kept Europe from exporting its balance of power system to the Americas.

By the end of the nineteenth century the Europeans (and now Japanese), lusting for colonies and racing to build blue-water navies, threatened again to encroach on America's sphere. So a second burst of strategic creativity occurred between 1880 and 1910, when the Naval War College, progressive businessmen, and internationalists such as Theodore Roosevelt adjusted to the era of industrial imperialism with a modern two-ocean fleet, the open-door policy, and support of the balance of power abroad (viz., TR's mediation of the Russo-Japanese War).

The third burst of strategic thinking occurred, of course, between 1947 and 1953, when the Communist threat inspired the Truman administration to adopt Containment and the Eisenhower administration to draft a plan (NSC 162/2) to wage the Cold War without the United States going bankrupt, becoming a garrison state, or bleeding to death in brushfire wars such as Korea. To be sure, a succession of storms buffeted the U.S. ship of state and forced it to correct its charted course. Sputnik discredited Ike's massive retaliation, Vietnam besmirched Kennedy's and Johnson's flexible response and counterinsurgency, Americans on the left and right rebelled against Nixon's realpolitik, and the Iranian revolution and Soviet invasion of Afghanistan put paid to Carter's human rights approach. But Americans continued to adjust, recoup, and rebound until, under Reagan and Bush, George Kennan's prophesy was fulfilled and the Soviet Union collapsed from its own contradictions and overextension.

In each of these eras, the United States faced clear and present dangers. In each of them a distinguished "aristocracy" of Wise Men assessed the global environment, responded with prudent designs, and won the support of successive Congresses and administrations. But what about the times in between? Did the United States have no strategy at all in the mid-nineteenth century, during the world wars of the twentieth century, or since 1991? The answer to that is no: during those eras the United States pursued what amounted to *antistrategies*. That is, the administrations of Wilson, Hoover, Franklin Roosevelt, to some extent Carter, and certainly Clinton did not assess the global environment in order to draft strategy. Rather, they attempted to *transform* the global environment in such a way as to make traditional strategy unnecessary. Whether the vehicle was the Wilsonian vision of disarmament, self-determination, and collective security, the isolationism of FDR's first term or the United Nations plan of his third, or the conversion of all nations to the American Way through globalization and enlargement, the United States has repeatedly tried to purge the world of strategic competition.[10]

Given the revolutions and wars plaguing the world throughout the twentieth century, Wilson and his later disciples had good reason to conclude that the United States must control events "over there" if it was to remain free to build its future "over here." But the antistrategies pursued in the name of that American mission have invariably failed because they contain three logical flaws and one pronounced danger. The first flaw is that if America is truly exceptional, then by definition its ideals are *sui generis* and will not be embraced, or interpreted in the same way, by any other nation (except, perhaps, Britain). Second, any attempt to pressure or persuade other nations—each of which cherishes its own history, culture, and interests—to submit to the latest U.S.

10. In David C. Henricksen's words ("In Our Own Image: The Sources of American Conduct in World Affairs," *The National Interest* [winter 1997/98]: 9–21): "When Americans came to the realization in the twentieth century that North America could no longer be a world unto itself, they searched for associations and partners that would 'domesticate' or 'constitutionalize' the anarchy of the state system" (p. 12).

design is bound, from their perspectives, to resemble the very imperialism America purports to oppose. Third, any success the United States may achieve in its campaign to control change abroad ipso facto makes it either the court of first appeal or else the outright enemy of any aggrieved nation or group anywhere. Hence, the danger is that the United States will inevitably be blamed by *someone* whether or not it intervenes in a conflict, and its arrogance will be repaid with enmity.

Talleyrand's diplomatic dictum was *"surtout pas trop de zêle"* (above all, not too much zeal), and the dangers of violating it deserve further mention below. But first, let us hear from today's exponents of an antistrategic American mission.

The Clintonian Vision of Globalization

So far, two schools of thought have dominated the debate over how to exploit the "unipolar moment" to advance America's national interests and values, which both camps assume to be identical and to serve all humanity. The first, the neoliberal vision, had been tenaciously pursued by the Clinton administration.[11] In his first foreign policy speech, Clinton referred to the aftermath of the two world wars to warn against isolationism: if engagement was needed then, then a fortiori it is even more needed now when trade, capital, services, and information ("the king of the world economy") have all become global. Referring to Somalia and Bosnia, he concluded: "If we could make a garden of democracy and prosperity and free enterprise in every part of this globe, the world would be a safer and a better and a more prosperous place for the United States and for all of you to raise your children in."[12]

In the Fall of 1993, Secretary of State Warren Christopher, National Security Adviser Anthony Lake, and UN Ambassador Madeleine

11. The quotations that follow are drawn from *The Clinton Foreign Policy Reader. Presidential Speeches With Commentary*, ed. Alvin Z. Rubinstein, Albina Shayevich, and Boris Zlotnikov (Armonk, N.Y.: M. E. Sharpe, 2000).
12. Speech at American University, 29 February 1993 (pp. 8–13).

Albright laid out the administration's vision in a series of speeches that set forth enlargement of the zones of democracy and market economy as the American goal, and assertive multilateralism the means. According to Lake, American values are universal and "we should not oppose using our military forces for humanitarian purposes," while Clinton told the UN that "our overriding purpose must be to expand and strengthen the world's community of market-based democracies." To be sure, after the Somalia debacle and the Republican takeover of Congress, the White House hedged its bets. "When our national security interests are threatened, we will, as America always has, use diplomacy when we can, but force if we must. We will act with others when we can, but alone when we must. We recognize, however, that while force can defeat an aggressor, it cannot solve underlying problems. Democracy and economic prosperity can take root in a struggling society only through local solutions carried out by the society itself. We therefore will send American troops abroad only when our interests are sufficiently at stake."[13] But the new guidelines did not prevent the president from waging two wars against Yugoslavia and occupying Bosnia and Kosovo in the name of multicultural state-building.

Meanwhile, U.S. relations with the two most important powers foundered. Clinton embraced Boris Yeltsin and claimed a strategic partnership with Russia, but was unwilling or unable to assist Russian democratization and economic recovery—"I know and you know that ultimately the history of Russia will be written by Russians"—while his drift toward a policy aimed at NATO expansion was considered a betrayal by Moscow. To be sure, Clinton's spin on NATO expansion was that "this new NATO will work with Russia, not against it. . . . We are determined to create a future in which European security is not a zero-sum game." He asserted that NATO must expand eastward to secure

13. Address to the UN (27 September 1993), p. 16, and Annual Report for 1995, p. 6.

democracy in Eastern Europe and "erase the line that Stalin drew."[14] But the Russians saw none of this as "nonzero-sum," called the war against Serbia a NATO aggression, and concluded that enlargement offered them nothing but humiliation.

Clinton also named China a strategic partner, throttling back the human rights crusade that began in his 1992 campaign and stressing trade and engagement. But instead, the United States and China have behaved like two clumsy boxers, feeling each other out, probing for weaknesses, and trying to gauge how willing the other may be to sacrifice his values and interests on the altar of greed. Still, the themes of Clintonian antistrategy come across clearly in speeches. In 1994 he granted that human rights abuses continued in China, not least in Tibet. But he concluded that "extending MFN will avoid isolating China and instead permit us to engage the Chinese with not only economic contacts but with cultural, educational, and other contacts and with a continuing aggressive effort in human rights." He sounded the theme of isolation repeatedly. "We must not seek to isolate ourselves from China. We will engage with China, without illusion." And again: "We will not change our policy in a way that isolates China from the global forces that have begun to empower the Chinese people to change their society and build a better future." When Chinese are present he was careful to add, "Of course, China will choose its own destiny."[15] But the logic behind engagement is that globalization and America's "soft power" will eventually roll back Communist rule in China.

14. Remarks to the American Society of Newspaper Editors (1 April 1993), pp. 51–56; Remarks at Signing of NATO-Russia Founding Act (27 May 1997), pp. 65–66; Commencement Address, U.S. Military Academy (31 May 1997), pp. 95–97.

15. Press Conference (26 May 1994), pp. 112–13; Remarks to Pacific Basin Economic Council (20 May 1996), pp. 114–18; Speech to the National Geographic Society (11 June 1998), pp. 127–31; Speech to the U.S. Institute of Peace (7 April 1999), pp. 132–38; Speech on the eve of President Jiang Zemin's visit (24 October 1997), pp. 119–26.

The Balkans may be recorded as the scene of the Clinton's administration's most egregious and enduring blunders: egregious because there the United States did not lead, but entered the fray reluctantly and too late to prevent the worst suffering, reverting to the same sort of utopian state-building the administration swore off after Somalia; and enduring because our generals in the Balkans now say that NATO forces will probably remain there for at least a decade.

How did Clinton justify his shifting response to the violence in the former Yugoslavia? In 1995, at the time of the Dayton Accords, he boasted of having resisted those who "were urging immediate intervention in the conflict" because "I decided that American ground troops should not fight a war in Bosnia because the United States cannot force peace on Bosnia's warring groups." But now that an accord had been reached, he would contribute twenty thousand American troops. By the end of 1997 it became clear that so far as "forcing peace" was concerned there was no light at the end of the tunnel. Then, when the Serbs' "ethnic cleansing" in Kosovo became intolerable, the President offered the opposite spin, urging swift action: "Sarajevo, the capital of neighboring Bosnia, is where World War I began. World War II and the Holocaust engulfed this region. In both wars, Europe was slow to recognize the dangers, and the United States waited even longer to enter the conflicts. Just imagine if leaders back then had acted wisely and early enough, how many lives could have been saved, how many Americans would not have had to die." His wild historical analogies aside (Milosevic does not equal Hitler, Serbia does not equal Germany, the Europe of 1999 does not equal the armed camps of 1914, and far *more* Americans would have died in the world wars had we entered at once), Clinton later admitted to a delayed response in Bosnia and called for NATO initiatives that put a "lasting peace and stability in Kosovo."[16] But at the end of the twentieth century, the ethnic

16. White House Address to the Nation (24 March 1999), pp. 190–93. Even the charges of "genocide" were outlandish: the forced exodus of Kosovars was the result,

hatreds there were as intractable as ever, and the Kosovo Liberation Army (once damned as a terrorist organization by Washington) is still determined to purge the province of Serbs and attach it to Albania.

It is easy to point out the contradictions in Clinton's foreign policy rhetoric. He insisted that the aim of American policy is to enlarge the sphere of democracy and markets, yet said with reference to Russia and China, Iraq, Iran, Serbia, and Cuba, that societies cannot be changed from without and must write their own history. He called for humanitarian interventions, yet admitted that force cannot remove the underlying causes of ethnic conflict. He promised to dispatch U.S. forces only when the national interest was at stake, yet implied that the national interest is *always* at stake because the spread of democracy is the surest way to enhance U.S. peace and prosperity. He rued all isolation as the enemy of peace and freedom, yet called on the UN "to isolate states and people who traffic in terror."[17] Above all, he insisted that the United States respect all religions and cultures, yet expected that globalization would overcome all cultural resistance to the universal values cherished by Americans.

Therein lies the core of conviction that allowed Clinton to equivocate in matters of tactics. "From his vantage point in the bully pulpit, Bill Clinton serves as chief evangelist for the gospel of globalization."[18] To be sure, he said, the post–Cold War world poses many dangers — regional wars, terrorism, proliferation of weapons of mass destruction, to name just a few — any of which "will undermine open markets, overwhelm open societies, and undercut our own prosperity."[19] But so long as the lid is kept on, victory is assured: "Armed with photocopiers and fax machines, e-mail and the Internet, and supported by an in-

---

not the cause, of the NATO bombing campaign, and occupying forces discovered only 2,108 Albanian corpses (*Wall Street Journal* [31 December 1999], A1, A12).

17. Cited by Rubinstein, *Clinton Foreign Policy Reader*, p. 158.

18. Andrew J. Bacevich, "The World According to Clinton," *First Things* (June–July 1999): 26–30 (quote, p. 27).

19. Speech on Foreign Policy, San Francisco (26 February 1999), pp. 36–42.

creasingly important community of non-governmental organizations, [oppressed peoples] will make their demands known, spreading the spirit of freedom, which as the history of the last ten years has shown us, ultimately will prevail."[20]

Clinton solved none of the post–Cold War problems he inherited, be it the future of Russia's democracy, nuclear arms, and economy; relations with China and Taiwan; the survival of Castro and Kim Jong-il; the stalemate with Iran and Iraq; the Indo-Pakistani conflict; the drug cartels and insurgency in Colombia; illegal immigration; the correct size and posture of the U.S. military; or the quagmire of humanitarian interventions (when, where, for what, and by whom?). But if Clinton was right, the way to manage such issues is precisely to temporize in the belief that a crisis that neither sparks a war nor wrecks the economy is a crisis surmounted—because the days of all bad guys are numbered.

Indeed, the neoliberal stance starts with the assumption that the Information Revolution and globalization are irreversible, that prosperity automatically spawns democracy, and that democracies never make war on each other. If such is the case, the United States need not do anything more than ensure that computer engineers and capital managers enjoy a free hand, and cajole all nations to accept the rules of the game drafted by the WTO, IMF, and World Bank. It is beside the point to fret about the war-fighting readiness of the U.S. armed forces because under the Clintonian dispensation, the military has no role save to serve as global police, while our diplomats' role is to cut deals with their counterparts as if they were already members of some global parliament drafting laws for mankind.

20. Speech to the UN General Assembly (22 September 1997), pp. 160–62.

The Neo-Conservative Crusade

The second school of thought on America's role in the post–Cold War is that of the neoconservatives, who disagree with neoliberals in two major respects. First, whereas Clintonians believe that history must move forward on the strength of ineluctable forces and that the United States need only play the role of policeman and banker, the neoconservatives believe that history needs help. The United States must play the role of a militant crusader lest global progress goes into reverse. Second, whereas Clintonians believe that American society is virtuous and progressive, and its foreign policy a reflection of that, the neoconservatives believe that American society is decadent, and hope that a virtuous foreign policy might serve to reform it. In operational terms, however, both schools imagine a harmonious world composed of capitalist democracies and differ only in their judgment as to how much force is required to realize it.

The neoconservative crusade was first preached in the run-up to the 1996 presidential election, when Bill Kristol and Bob Kagan called for a "neo-Reaganite foreign policy" designed to establish an American "benevolent global hegemony." Indeed, when the Russians and Chinese denounce "hegemonism," they say, Americans should "take it as a compliment and guide to action." Recalling the success of Reagan's rearmament and ideological offensive against the Soviet Union, they warn that Americans will throw away their Cold War victory if they do not reverse the decline in the military budget, intervene early and often against rogue states and terrorist groups that threaten the peace, and campaign aggressively on behalf of democracy. Accordingly, they chastise conservatives who cite John Quincy Adams's admonition against "going abroad in search of monsters to destroy." Why not? they ask. "The alternative is to leave monsters on the loose, ravaging and pillaging to their heart's content, as Americans stand by and watch. . . . [A] policy of sitting atop a hill and leading by example becomes in practice a policy of cowardice and dishonor." Finally, they reject fears dating from the Vietnam era that forceful state-building abroad might corrupt America, and assert that the "remoralization of America at home ultimately requires the remoralization of American foreign policy."[21]

Kristol, Kagan, and their colleagues David Brooks and Lawrence Kaplan won influential converts including Norman Podhoretz, but most conservatives resisted their call to arms. "Over the past four or five years," wrote Kagan, "a new pessimism, a new indifference, and even a new distaste for the promotion of democracy abroad have rippled through intellectual circles and out into the political arena." He had in mind Samuel Huntington's and Robert Kaplan's predictions of a clash of civilizations and the spread of chaos, which implied that large parts of the world would not embrace American values. Other conservatives questioned the desirability of democracy in the absence of checks and balances and the rule of law. But Kagan regarded such equivocation as a denial of America's essence and mission, and a threat to its domestic tranquillity. "Anyone worried about our national identity, and about the challenge posed to it by the balkanization of our culture, must know that we can hardly expect to unite our own country if we decide that those principles apply only in a few, rare circumstances and to a limited number of fortunate peoples." He completed his indictment of fainthearted conservatives by noting what a tragedy it would be "if, out of boredom, laziness, carelessness, or unfounded gloom," Americans failed to seize the opportunity bestowed by hegemony.[22]

Exploiting their access to the media, the neoconservatives continually revised their sermons in search of the right metaphors, role models, and scolds to reunite the 1980s Cold War coalition. When their invocation of Reagan did not work (critics said they distorted the history

21. William Kristol and Robert Kagan, "Toward a Neo-Reaganite Foreign Policy," *Foreign Affairs* (July–August 1996): 18–32.

22. Robert Kagan, "Democracies and Double Standards," *Commentary* (August 1997): 19–26.

and lessons of the Reagan era), they turned to Theodore Roosevelt and the theme of "national greatness."[23] When TR did not do the trick (critics noted his big government philosophy and treason against the Republican party), they resorted to fire and brimstone: "There is no middle ground between a decline in U.S. power, a rise in world chaos, and a dangerous 21st century, on the one hand, and a Reaganite reassertion of American power and moral leadership, on the other. Some Republicans think that what is needed is merely better 'management' of foreign policy, a more 'adult' approach to the world. But they are wrong."[24] Frustrated again, they resorted to the unkindest cut of all by accusing their conservative critics of "leftism."[25] Finally, they dropped the rhetorical equivalent of an atomic bomb by resurrecting the phrase "clear and present danger" and naming their fellow conservatives today's "present danger" by dint of their "absentmindedness, or parsimony, or indifference" to world peace and liberal democracy. "The middle path many of our political leaders prefer, with token increases in the defense budget and a 'humble' view of America's role in the world, will not suffice."[26]

Like the neoliberals, neoconservatives also imagine that blessed dawn when the world will bask in what political scientists call "the democratic peace." But they do not believe in the power of globalization alone to dislodge tyrants, and suspect that engagement amounts to appeasement. To them, there are monsters still to destroy, so the United States must deploy far larger armed forces, a feisty ideology, and a robust diplomacy. It must pursue a traditional strategy for the

23. William Kristol and David Brooks, "What Ails Conservatism," *Wall Street Journal* (15 September 1997), p. A22.

24. William Kristol and Robert Kagan, "Foreign Policy and the Republican Future," *The Weekly Standard* (7 September 1998).

25. Lawrence F. Kaplan, "Leftism on the Right: Conservatives Learn to Blame America First," *The Weekly Standard* (9 February 1998): 27–29.

26. Robert Kagan and William Kristol, "The Present Danger," *The National Interest* (spring 2000): 57–69.

ultimate purpose of transcending strategy, which explains the neoconservatives' tireless efforts to rally Americans to gird up and lead the global parade.

Debunking the "Neos"

What is one to make of all this? Is the theological millennium about to arrive coincident with the Gregorian calendar? Will stock markets always go up, the New Economy never cease to be new, and OOTWs (operations other than war) remain the worst contingency the Pentagon need prepare for? To read Thomas Friedman one would believe it so.[27] According to him no government on earth can resist the will of the "electronic herd," those nameless and stateless managers of investment capital funds who move billions of dollars into developing markets that meet their demands for transparency, low taxes, repatriation of profits, and political propriety, while conversely destroying through capital flight any regime that shuns their demands. But Friedman's harmonious, unified world, however popular it may be among the denizens of Renaissance Weekends, is still mythical, because if it were real, then economic, social, and political conditions around the world would be increasingly uniform. Instead, we witness a widening gap between the haves and have-nots, expensive bailouts to keep even aspiring "haves" from collapsing, and growing resentment of the "herd" and its presumed patron, the United States. According to Kenneth Waltz, "Globalization is the fad of the 1990s, and globalization is made in America."[28] But in its name the post–Cold War global order is taking on the characteristics of a Monopoly game in which the rich and clever

27. Thomas Friedman, *The Lexus and the Olive Tree* (New York: Farrar, Straus, Giroux, 1999). See also John Micklethwait and Adrian Wooldridge, *A Future Perfect: The Challenge and Hidden Promise of Globalization* (New York: Crown Publishers, 2000), and Susan Strange, *The Retreat of the State: The Diffusion of Power in the World Economy* (New York: Cambridge University Press, 2000).

28. Kenneth N. Waltz, "Globalization and American Power," *The National Interest* (spring 2000): 46–56.

always win, but the poor and stupid cannot be permitted to lose. So if they go bankrupt, the American bank with the bottomless vault bails them out; if they break a rule, the American cop says "Go to jail." And so far it has worked. But if and when the U.S. economy tanks and the supply of new loans for the losers dries up, globalization will be revealed as a grand Ponzi scheme.

In other words, to dispense with a national strategy out of faith that the natural play of material forces will create a new Global Man and that nation-states will "wither away," as the neoliberals advocate, is to embrace a Marxism with American characteristics. But the historian in me says that the world today is in a highly *unnatural* state that is maintained, like an excited atom in a cloud chamber, only by constant, expensive inputs of energy. And nowhere is this expenditure of energy more evident than in U.S. military deployments. Had natural patterns prevailed, the United States would have scaled back in the absence of any clear and present dangers abroad. Instead, it plays "Globocop" in the name of an even more ambitious agenda than it pursued while the Soviet Union existed.[29] Then, our purpose was just to make the world safe for democracy. Now, our mission is to make the world democratic, which in theory requires the sanctioning, bombing, or occupying of any country that backslides. As a result, the U.S. defense budget accounts for one-third—and the U.S. and its allies *four-fifths*—of all the military spending on earth. By comparison, Russia and China are virtual pacifists. Yet, in spite of such spending, U.S. forces are so overstretched that recruitment and retainment suffer badly, and morale is abysmal.

What is the justification for the deployments to Somalia, Bosnia, Kosovo, Haiti, the South China Sea, South Korea, the Persian Gulf, and Europe? Is it to promote human rights and prevent wars and ethnic cleansing? Why then does the United States ignore the strife in

29. See George Szamuely, "Globocop: When the United States Becomes Dirty Harry," *American Outlook* (summer 1998): 9–14.

Rwanda, Sudan, Congo, Eritrea, Afghanistan, Sri Lanka, Indonesia, Fiji, and Kashmir? All told, some thirty wars rage in the world that have taken nine million lives and created thirty million refugees. So some absolute morality is obviously not the measuring stick for U.S. interventions. Is the motive to promote the Wilsonian principle of national self-determination? Hardly, because five thousand ethnic groups exist on the globe, but only 185 states. To promise self-determination for all "oppressed minorities" would multiply global chaos a thousandfold. Is it to teach the inhabitants of a few favored countries to forge peaceful, multicultural democracies? If so, it has not worked in the Balkans or, for that matter, in the United States. Indeed, no example damns the global meliorist impulse more effectively than America herself. How can our federal government claim to have the resources, power, prestige, technology, wisdom, altruism, and not least the right to remake other societies in our image, when that same government has failed, despite billions of dollars in social programs, to improve the lot of America's own inner cities? We should not be surprised that an increasing number of economists and journalists have found that foreign aid invariably harms recipient nations, and that American state-building projects invariably fail, from our colony in the Philippines, to South Vietnam, Somalia, the Balkans, Haiti (three times), and most recently Sierra Leone, where American meddling again made matters worse.[30]

Nor is democracy devoutly to be wished in all cases, as the neoconservatives would have it. As Robert Kaplan observes, democracies are value-neutral and "do not always make societies more civil." Who really wants to see "democracy" topple the conservative Arab monarchies? Indeed, "the very fact that we retreat to moral arguments—and often moral arguments only—to justify democracy indicates that for

---

30. On the latest fiascos see "How U.S. Left Sierra Leone Tangled in a Curious Web," *New York Times* (4 June 2000), p. 6, and Stephen Johnson, "The Administration's Failed Gamble in Haiti," Heritage Foundation Executive Memorandum (19 May 2000).

many parts of the world the historical and social arguments supporting democracy are just not there."[31] And American moralism can be hard to swallow. The United States itself was founded through ethnic cleansing. The United States oppressed various minorities for most of its history. The United States grew its economy through "sweatshop" labor and tariff protectionism. And the United States *invented* weapons of mass destruction. None of that is meant as a judgment, much less an endorsement of such practices by others; it is simply historical fact that helps to explain why so many people abroad question our "exceptional" values. Russians, Chinese, and Southeast Asians denounce enlargement as a form of imperialism and claim superiority for Orthodox or Asian values. Europeans and Asians resent demands that they lower barriers to trade or adjust their labor policies to suit politically correct Americans. Islamic and Catholic nations are offended by American preachments on reproductive and family issues, and are appalled by the pornography, nihilism, and materialism invading them over the Internet. Brazil and other developing countries resist the U.S. environmental agenda, and American nuclear and missile controls anger China, India, Pakistan, Iran, and other states jealous of their sovereign right of self-defense. To all it seems that an America that extols diversity and multiculturalism at home has no tolerance for them where other countries are concerned.

A final hypocrisy of the global do-gooders, of course, is that they are only prepared to lecture and bomb small and defenseless peoples who cannot inflict casualties on their tormentors. The Russians, Chinese, and North Koreans remain free to oppress dissidents without fear of American lightning bolts.

Neoconservatives mostly agree that U.S. interventions to date have been selective, late, and of dubious success. They rued Clinton's "appeasement" of authoritarian regimes, failure to prevent calamity in the

---

31. Robert D. Kaplan, "Was Democracy Just a Moment?" *The Atlantic Monthly* (December 1997): 55–80 (quote, p. 60).

Balkans and elsewhere, and loss of leverage over Iraq. But rather than questioning interventionism, their solution is to intervene sooner, more often, with more firepower even as they "dodge the central foreign question facing America"—how to craft policy that involves "neither a crusading activism that mindlessly diffuses vital resources nor an isolationism that eschews important opportunities to shape events."[32]

Finally, the more coercion the United States employs to overcome the mounting resistance to its global agenda, the more enemies it manufactures and the greater the risk of Americans becoming the target of terrorism. "If much of the Yugoslav Republic lies in ruins," wrote Michael Hirsch, "so too is America's reputation as the Gentle Hegemon." Why hasn't the sole superpower been victorious in its ongoing crusade? The reason, Hirsch suggests, "is 'blowback.' That is an old spook term for U.S. policies that backfire on Americans at home."[33] Chalmers Johnson goes so far as to argue that the United States has become a "rogue superpower" raining down ordnance with no accountability. In the short run, he predicts, this will magnify blowback; in the long run it will cause the overstretched American empire to crash in the same fashion as the Soviet empire, and for the same reasons.[34]

"Besotted with ambition, empires in our age have betrayed an astonishing propensity for self-inflicted wounds," writes Andrew Bacevich, who fears the United States has forgotten that "great moral lesson of imperial hubris." Neoliberals pursue hegemony by indirection, while neoconservatives are up front about it, oblivious to the fact that "benign hegemony" is a contradiction in terms and that the empire

32. Kim R. Holmes and John Hillen, "Misreading Reagan's Legacy: A Truly Conservative Foreign Policy," *Foreign Affairs* (September/October 1996): 162–67 (quote, p. 163).

33. Michael Hirsch, "At War with Ourselves," *Harper's Magazine* (July 1999): 60–69 (quote, p. 60).

34. Chalmers Johnson, *Blowback: The Costs and Consequences of American Empire* (New York: Henry Holt, 2000).

America offers is singularly devoid of moral substance. "One reads about the world's desire for American leadership only in the United States," a British diplomat has remarked. "Everywhere else one reads about American arrogance and unilateralism."[35]

Some "neos" will no doubt dismiss McDougall for a curmudgeon, perhaps speculating that my evident bitterness as a Vietnam veteran has so clouded my historian's judgment that I cannot see how much the world has changed. If that is what they are thinking, they err again. Obviously this era is unique—all eras are unique—and new horizons certainly beckon. But some things, such as human nature, do not change, as one glimpse into a distant mirror should prove.

A Homily on Pope Urban II

The eleventh century—the first of that new millennium—was the best and worst of times for Europe.[36] On the one hand, the Dark Ages had ended, the marauding Vikings and Normans were being assimilated, and the marchlands of Bohemia, Hungary, and Poland were tamed and converted. Agriculture was booming, thanks to the mouldboard plough, towns and commerce were sprouting, and Europe was primed for the creative outburst of the High Middle Ages. On the other hand, Latin Christendom was torn by dissent and new heresies, corruption among clergy, and the incessant fighting of knights bereft of foreign foes. French kings were helpless to enforce royal authority against feuding vassals, while the Holy Roman Emperors challenged papal authority by attempting to tax the church and name bishops. The popes flung excommunications in all directions, ordered priestly celibacy, and insisted on Rome's primacy to the point of schism with the Orthodox church. But nothing worked until Urban II hit on the idea of a Crusade

---

35. Andrew J. Bacevich, "The Irony of American Power," *First Things* (March 1998): 19–27; Waltz, "Globalization and American Power," pp. 55–56.

36. The following section was read to The Philadelphia Society (24 April 1999), and published in *Orbis* (summer 1999): 346–54.

as a way to ameliorate all of Europe's problems at once. Through a Crusade he could reassert papal authority, reimpose orthodoxy, divert the restless knights abroad, and forge in Europe a unity unknown since the breakup of Charlemagne's empire.

What is more, it appeared to work. The chroniclers in the Holy Land marveled at the Crusaders' penitent demeanor, as if they constituted "a military monastery on the move," and the knights so recently condemned as lustful brutes were transformed by troubadours into heroes of faith. The home front rallied with such enthusiasm that Urban had to prohibit clergy and women from taking up arms themselves. Meanwhile, the Cluniac reform movement inspired monks to return to work, prayer, and abstinence, and encouraged the laity to do likewise.

Similarly, the pacifist movement, which condemned war among Christians, rushed to endorse wars waged "in defense of righteousness." And Pope Urban, who hated armies until he found a use for them, became the most eager interventionist of all, justifying the Crusade as a "war of liberation." Ever since St. Augustine, war has been considered just only if tempered by love of one's enemy, as when loving parents punish children for their own good. But Urban did not ask the Crusaders to love the Saracens; he asked only that they not be moved by glory or gain. So deployment of force was permitted even in a spirit of vengeance—so long as self-interest was not involved.

Think what we have learned so far. First, the Crusade was deemed acceptable because it employed force in the absence of any national interest. Second, the Crusade was needed to reforge a Western alliance that was crumbling in the absence of real threats: Europe must go out of area or out of business. Third, the Crusade was sold as a moral cause serving the enlargement of Western Civilization. Fourth, an ulterior motive of the Crusade was to remoralize the home front and restore its greatness. Fifth, the Crusade was designed to elevate the Church above all particular interests so that it might exercise, as it were, a benevolent hegemony.

We know the real results of the Crusades: huge expenditures; immense loss of life among Christians, Muslims, pagans, and heretics; assaults on Jewish communities; forcible conversions in violation of canon law; and all manner of impure motives on the part of the knights. Plunder became the primary goal of several crusades, climaxing in the sack of Constantinople in 1204, and imperialism the goal of others, as when Crusaders dreamed of conquering Egypt and Syria. And rather than moralizing the home front, the Crusades served as a conduit for the import of Islamic, gnostic, and pagan ideas. Later Crusaders yearned to go east just to indulge their own vices, as the Aquitaine knight who "went with many others to Jerusalem, but contributed nothing to the Christian cause. He was a fervent womanizer and for that reason showed himself to be inconstant in all that he did." His name was William.[37]

What did it all achieve? The Latin kingdom in the Holy Land, an outlandish example of state building, lasted only eighty-eight years. But success no longer mattered, because crusading became a systematic part of the political, social, and religious structure of Europe—a mediator, safety valve, and justification to mobilize force for all sorts of institutional purposes. The thirteenth century scholar Hostiensis even advanced "the revolutionary idea that Christendom had an intrinsic right to extend its sovereignty over all who did not recognize the rule of the Roman Church."[38]

No one speaks of crusading today. Advocates of benevolent hegemony and what Tony Blair calls "the humanitarian war" militantly insist that U.S. foreign policy be both moral and forceful, yet they shy from the word "crusade." It calls to mind politically incorrect vices such as intolerance, hypocrisy, violence, and greed—and politically

37. Jonathan Riley-Smith, *The First Crusade and the Idea of Crusading* (London: Athlone Press, 1986), pp. 17–18.

38. Louise and Jonathan Riley-Smith, *The Crusades. Idea and Reality* (London: Edward Arnold, 1981), p. 29.

incorrect virtues such as chivalry, gallantry, sacrifice, and faith. But the reflection we see in the Medieval mirror is not only real, it is familiar and unbecoming. It tells us that to be a crusader in theory means to go far afield to fight, selflessly, for a righteous cause, but that to preach a crusade in fact means to cloak with morality what is really a ploy to shore up a leader's authority, distract attention from conflicts at home, forge artificial unity within a flagging alliance, or pursue economic advantage — unless, of course, one really believes that globalization, the new world order, and American hegemony possess a teleological force equal to that claimed by Medieval Catholicism.

Of Grasshoppers and Ants

One need not be a disciple of Pat Buchanan to draw the right lessons from the fate of ideological empires. Since 1991, such staunch inter-nationalists as Jeane Kirkpatrick, Owen Harries, Jonathan Clarke, Henry Kissinger, Robert Kaplan, Michael Mandelbaum, Fareed Za-karia, Samuel Huntington, Adam Garfinkle, Charles Maynes, Charles Krauthammer, Kim Holmes, John Hillen, Andrew Bacevich, and Condoleezza Rice have all warned against excessive moralism, triumphalism, and militancy in our foreign relations. As Peter Rodman notes pithily: "Wilsonian presidents drive [other nations] crazy — and have done so ever since Woodrow Wilson."[39] We are indeed living in extraordinary times, the high summer of American power, and of course the United States must be a leader. But the most foolish thing we could do is to assume, like the grasshopper, that summer will never end, squandering our energies hopping about, turning allies into neutrals and neutrals into enemies with incessant chirping, and storing up nothing against the winter that will someday arrive.

That is why Americans ought to cease calling for the conversion of

---

39. Peter W. Rodman, *Uneasy Giant. The Challenges to American Predominance* (Washington, D.C.: The Nixon Center, 2000), p. 44.

all nations in this generation, as their missionaries did of old, and husband the *assets* they will need when and if strategic genius again becomes necessary. The ones on my A-list are these.[40]

(1) A strong U.S. economy subject only to mild recessions and modest inflation *whatever meltdowns should occur overseas.*

(2) A robust military endowed with superior technology and high morale, and designed to deter or win wars, *not "operations other than war."*

(3) Statesmanship, which is to say presidents with a prudent vision of U.S. security interests, the skill to communicate their vision at home and abroad, and the character to *spurn temptations to mortgage foreign policy to a political or personal agenda.*

(4) A bipartisan internationalist consensus in Congress, which should not be difficult to revive, but which is *easily dissipated by an executive too arrogant, insecure, or distracted* to give Congress the attention and consultation it needs.

(5) Sturdy regional alliances, because America's present dominance will be transitory—but alliances, too, need care and feeding, and nothing harms them so much as invoking them only when crises erupt, *asking them to do too little* (as if their members had few interests in common), *or insisting they do too much* (as if their members shared everything in common).

(6) Balances of power in Europe, the Middle East, and Asia, which means American efforts to help manage relations among Russia, China, Japan, India, Iran, Iraq and their neighbors, because *helping to prevent war among the big powers is the most moral task the U.S. can perform,* and because we cannot hope for soft landings in Korea, Taiwan, Central Asia, the Caucasus, and elsewhere if Washington is not on speaking terms with Beijing and Moscow.

(7) Finally, strong Pan-American institutions, because the *most*

40. The following list is drawn from a speech delivered to the Foreign Policy Research Institute (10 November 1999) and published in *Orbis* (spring 2000): 176–85.

predictable and direct challenges to U.S. security are the invasion of illegal immigrants and drugs, and the prospect of civil collapse in Colombia, Mexico, and the lands in between.

Note that nowhere on the list do free trade (the neoliberal mantra) and democracy (the neoconservative one) appear. I am for them, by and large, but I know the United States can live without their triumph abroad so long as the seven assets above are in place. But remove any of those assets—imagine the U.S. economy in reverse, a weak or demoralized military, a floundering president, a divided, partisan Congress, a crack-up of NATO, a Europe or Asia gripped by wars cold or hot, or an America beset by crises on its southern frontier—and the United States will be severely handicapped when and if something big does need doing.

That is not to say the United States should cease proclaiming its ideals. But without quiet strength and a dose of humility it will become a ridiculous caricature of itself, discredit its ideals in the eyes of the world, only weakening itself. That is the grasshopper mode: peripatetic, noisy, hopping into other people's backyards, and unready when the weather turns nasty. Ants, by contrast, are admired for their unity, work, husbandry, and foresight, and for minding their own business unless their own hill is disturbed, in which case they pour forth as an army.

Kristol and Kagan are right about one thing. Americans themselves are the present danger, which is why the best admonitions for us today, in my judgment, are these.[41]

> *Powerful men and nations are in greater danger from their own illusions than from their neighbors' hostile designs.* —Reinhold Niebuhr

> *Lilies that fester smell worse than weeds, because the higher the pretensions of our rulers, the more meddlesome and impertinent their rule is likely to be, and the more the thing in whose name they rule will be defiled.* —C. S. Lewis

41. Niebuhr cited by Bacevich, "Irony of American Power," p. 27; C. S. Lewis, "Lilies That Fester," 157 *The Twentieth Century* (April 1955), pp. 340–41.

Index

regionalism: Africa, 42; Asia and Latin America and, 41–42; culture, national identity and, 46–47; European, 40–42; integration and, 34
religion, 51, 91; extremes of, 91; morals of different, 138
Republicans, 12–13
resistance: adversary, 27–28; environmental, 29; self-generated, 28–29
revolution, 22–23
rogue states, 49, 66, 96–103; different strategies against different, 112–13; restraint imposed on, 7–11
Roman empire, 1, 18–19
Roosevelt, Franklin, 27, 125
Roosevelt, Theodore, 134
Russia, 53, 73, 91, 92, 114, 144. *See also* USSR; bankruptcy of, 11; China and, 109; corruption in, 55, 104; democracy problems in, 59, 104, 131; diplomatic pressures of, 11; European democratic community and, 69; exporting of nuclear weapons by, 112; friction with U.S. and, 105; global aspirations of, 18, 106, 111; military spending of, 136; NATO expansion and, 127–28; post–Cold War, 94; radical Islam against, 11–12; U.S. cross purposes with, 5; U.S. loans to, 104, 106; U.S. unable to assist recovery of, 127
Rwanda, 1, 95–96

Santiago resolution, 68–69
security, intraregional, 41–42
self-regulation, 24, 37
Serbia, 7, 10–11, 12–13, 40, 41, 44, 91, 92, 98–101, 110, 127–28, 128–30, 137
Shiites, 97
social justice, 20, 25, 35
socialism, 40
Somalia, 43–44, 55, 95–96, 136, 137
South Asia, 92–95

South Korea, 10, 78–79, 85, 95, 102, 103, 108, 109
Soviet Union. *See* USSR
Spanish-American War, 3
specialization, 19, 20–21
starvation, 95
statecraft, 19, 144; values and, 25–26; within system, 23
strategy: anti, 125–26, 128; consensus and, 23; containment, 4, 5, 15, 17, 124; control of change and, 125–26; democracy, antithesis to long-term, 120–21; folly of debate on, 119–22; generalists and, 17–18, 20–21; instruction and, 23; operational level of, 119–20; reactive nature of, 120; reconciliation and, 121; secretiveness of, 119
strategy, grand: defining, 15, 17; delegation and, 24–25; destination specified in, 21–26; ecological, 32; higher purpose of, 25; historical, 123–24; lack of, 17–19, 18–19; liberal democracy as, 59; minimizing resistance in, 26–29; plan and improvise for, 29–32; reasons for, 18–21; threat as basis for, 1, 55, 59, 123
Sudan, 7
system, change of, 22–23

Taiwan, 92, 108, 131, 144
terrorism, 7, 49, 92–93
trade orientation indexes, 78–80, 82–83
Turkey, 51, 63

unilateralism, 25, 93, 140
United Nations: civil unrest and, 44; contempt of, 25; debt by U.S. to, 44; democratization of, 45–46; global parliament of, 46; increase of U.S. support to, 44–45, 47; inspections of, 97–98; international institutions and, 36; military/peacekeeping operations of, 43–44, 45, 95; Special